Faith BUILDER CATECHISM

Devotions to Level Up Your
Family Discipleship

BY KEVIN HIPPOLYTE, JARED KENNEDY, AND TREY KULLMAN

New Growth Press, Greensboro, NC 27401
Copyright © 2023 by Kevin Hippolyte, Jared Kennedy, Trey Kullman

Cover: FaceOut, Jeff Miller; imagery from Shutterstock
Illustration: Jeremy Slagle
Interior Design/Typesetting: Dan Stelzer

ISBN: 978-1-64507-290-4 (Print)
ISBN: 978-1-64507-291-1 (eBook)

LCCN: 2023043007

Printed in India
31 30 29 28 27 26 25 24   2 3 4 5 6

CONTENTS

CONTENTS

CONTENTS

CONTENTS

INTRODUCTION

The most enthralling video games take place in elaborate kingdoms. They have characters we embody and root for, as well as stories we connect with. Whether you're rescuing princesses with *Super Mario Bros.*, scoring goals on the latest FIFA game, or slicing up flying objects with your beat saber, players learn—clumsily at first and then with greater ease—to inhabit a video game's world.

All learning works this way. A kid doesn't jump straight into quadratic equations in their first math class. They first learn to count, then add, subtract, multiply, and divide. Once they've mastered the basics, they'll encounter the complexities of algebra, geometry, and calculus.

The same is true with our faith. We don't dive into the complexities of the Trinity with preschoolers. When building a Christian worldview, we first introduce kids to the basics of the Christian life by telling simple Bible stories, memorizing short verses, and rehearsing bedtime prayers.

Faith-Building through Catechism

One great tool that can help parents with the task of teaching the basics is a catechism. The word *catechism* comes from the Greek word *katācheō*, which means to teach or instruct. The Greek word is used for any kind of

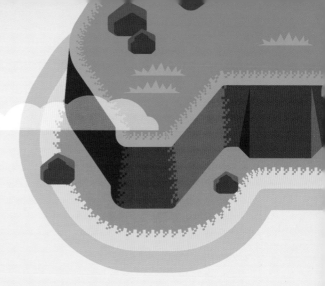

teaching or instruction (Luke 1:4; Acts 18:25), but early in church history it came to refer to new converts being taught the basics of Christianity by memorizing questions and answers about church doctrine and practice. Catechisms as they're used today are just that—a series of questions and answers used to teach basic Bible truth.

The roots of this method go even further back than the early church. When God delivered Israel from Egypt, he gave them laws, ceremonies, and sacrifices to help them remember his great rescue. At the time, God was nation-building, and he had the children of the nation in mind when he gave the Law. We can see this in the way God anticipated children's questions. In passages like Exodus 12:26–27; 13:14–16; and Joshua 4:6–7; we find a pattern like this one: "When your children ask you, 'What does this ceremony mean to you?' then tell them . . ."

God created kids with curiosity and a sense of wonder. When they asked questions about his laws or the Passover celebration, God wanted Israelite parents to be prepared. In each of these passages, he gave them a simple script for answering their kids' questions. In Exodus 12:27 ESV, the answer went like this: "It is the sacrifice of the LORD's Passover, for he passed over the houses of the people of Israel in Egypt, when he struck the Egyptians but spared our houses." God instructed parents to put this script to memory, so they'd always be ready with an answer—one that explained to their children how the annual celebration was rooted in God's big redemption plan.

Throughout Christian history, the best catechisms have majored on Christian basics as outlined in the Apostles' Creed, the Ten Commandments, and the Lord's Prayer. Such truths help kids learn what Dorothy Sayers describes as the "grammar" of the faith. The devotionals in this book follow this pattern. Building on the foundation of Martin Luther's *Small Catechism* (1529), the *Heidelberg Catechism* (1576), the *Westminster Shorter Catechism* (1642–47), and the *Catechism for Young Children* (1840), this book focuses on basic building blocks of our historic faith: God's glory, God's kingdom, the gospel, God's church, and his mission.

If we're honest, our kids are often catechized by YouTube, video games, and online streaming. But God wants them to be catechized in the beauty of his good news. He wants them to be immersed in the wonder of his great adventure. We can do this by engaging and rehearsing his truth together with our kids. We can build a foundation of faith by teaching deep theological concepts that apply the truth to their tech-saturated world.

Turn Off the Screens and Get Started

You may be a young parent taking first steps toward discipling your child, or you may be a seasoned pro who's already got weekly devotional rhythms in place. Whether the only spiritual direction you've given your kids is praying before meals, or even if you've never done that, this book is for you, and it couldn't be easier to use! Just set aside ten minutes once per week over a meal or before bedtime. Turn off the screens, and then pick up a Bible and your imagination. Begin building these big truths about Jesus into your child's life. Here are a few quick tips for how to make this time worthwhile.

 Don't be afraid to start early. The video game theme and devotionals in this book are designed for older grade school children and pre-teens. But kids can learn answers to catechism questions as soon as they begin to talk. By doing so, they will add to their vocabulary words that reflect biblical truth. You can begin the Bible memorization as early as a child's third birthday.

 Memorize questions, answers, and verses. It is helpful for kids to memorize the verses along with the questions and answers. This is a way of ensuring that catechism remains a gospel tool that can be used to point kids to Jesus and his redemptive story told in the Bible. Kids should learn that the Bible, not the catechism, is the foundation for our faith.

 Teach it "when you sit down." The fifty-two devotionals that accompany the catechism are intended to aid in planned times with your family. The question sections in the devotionals are designed to cultivate conversations. Turn off screens and put devices away so you can be fully present with one another. Both conversation and memorization require everyone's full attention.

 Teach it "along the road." The truth is that worldviews are often better caught than taught. That's because we learn best in the context of a relationship. Parents should always be alert for teachable moments—opportunities to talk about how the doctrine learned in the catechism applies to everyday life. The catechism is really just a reference point, a script that parents and children have put to memory that can be explained and applied through informal conversations.

Learn it with your church community. *Faith Builder Catechism* follows the pattern of the *Heidelberg Catechism*, providing one devotional that corresponds with each Sunday (or "Lord's Day") of the year. The questions, answers, and devotionals are organized into fifty-two divisions so a church community can work together to memorize short sections each week and repeat the full catechism annually.

Are you ready to move from screen time to deep discipleship? Gather your family and begin right now. Together, you will talk through many compelling truths. Each devotional includes discussion, reading, memorization, prayer, and review. Simply follow along and enjoy the journey.

NOTE: At the back of the book are stickers to use to track your progress through the catechism.

Let's get started!

LEVEL 1

GOD'S GLORY

Who made you and everything?

God made everything and me.

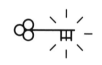

MEMORY VERSE:
In the beginning, God created the heavens and the earth. Genesis 1:1

Power-up Question:
What is your favorite video game?
Describe the world in which it takes place.

>>> READ GENESIS 1:1-31

When a man builds a house, he must first have wood, nails, glass, and many other things. If he does not have something out of which to make it, he cannot build a house. But God made the world out of nothing at all. —Catherine Vos

We see in Genesis 1 that God made everything. He made every kind of place—the mountains, rivers, forests, and oceans. He crafted every kind of plant—pine trees, bluegrass, rose bushes, and even the broccoli we eat (or avoid!). God made the seaweed that grows in the ocean. He made every kind of animal—giraffes, butterflies, aardvarks, and stingrays. And he made you and me.

When we make things, we use materials that we have on hand. If you want to make a piece of artwork, you use a blank piece of paper or a canvas. Then, you take crayons, markers, pencils, pens, or paint to create something on that blank page. You might even cut out clippings from a magazine and paste them into your masterpiece with glue. God didn't create that way. He didn't have any materials or supplies; there weren't any! Amazingly, God made everything out of nothing at all.

AMAZINGLY, GOD MADE EVERYTHING OUT OF NOTHING AT ALL.

God made everything and us just by speaking words. The first day began because God said, "Let there be light." God spoke, and what God spoke happened. It's hard to imagine because we can't make things with just words. But, when God speaks, his Word creates new things.

THINK ABOUT IT

- When you create something in a video game, what materials do you use? Who provides them? How is that different with God?

- If you could create things with just words, what would you make?

>>> PRAY: *God, thank you for all the wonderful things you've made—ice cream, video games, grass and trees, animals, and even us. Amen.*

What is God like?

God is our loving and almighty Creator.

Does God have a beginning?

No. He has no beginning and no end.
He is forever.

MEMORY VERSE:
Lord, our Lord, how majestic is your name in all
the earth! You have set your glory in the heavens.
Psalm 8:1

Power-up Question:
If you could design a video game
character, what would they be like?
What's your inspiration?

>>> READ PSALM 8

People build rocket ships to fly above the atmosphere and to the moon and Mars. We send satellites to the edges of our solar system, and we build telescopes to see beyond our galaxy. People have never traveled to the edge of the universe, but, even if we could, God is still bigger. The Bible says, "O Lord, our Lord, your majestic name fills the earth! Your glory is higher than the heavens" (Psalm 8:1 NLT). Our majestic God is perfectly powerful. He's not limited by time or space or ability. He sees what happened at the beginning of time, and he knows what will happen at the end. Because God is mighty and eternal, he doesn't need us. God is perfect and full of joy—all by himself.

But God still thought about us. He carefully crafted us as characters in his big story. He chose to make us. He's given us bodies and souls, eyes and ears, a brain to think, and hands to feel. He takes care of our daily needs—clothes to wear, a bed to sleep in, family and friends. Every good gift we have comes from God.

EVERY GOOD GIFT YOU HAVE COMES FROM GOD.

Why does the almighty God, who doesn't need anything, give us so much? Do we earn or deserve his love? No way! God gives us all these mercies simply because he's our loving and merciful Father. Because of this, we thank him, serve him, and obey him.

THINK ABOUT IT

• How do you feel when you remember the truth that the almighty God loves you and thinks about you?

>>> **PRAY:** *God, you are big and mighty. Thank you for thinking about and loving us. Thank you for sharing your joy with us when you didn't have to. Amen.*

Are there more gods than one?

No. There is only one true God.

MEMORY VERSE:
Hear, O Israel: The Lord our God, the Lord is one. Deuteronomy 6:4

Power-up Question:
What is your favorite video gaming system? Why?

>>> READ 1 KINGS 18:16-46

> *God is distinct in His deity . . . God says, "Don't make any likeness of me, because anything you come up with will make me look bad."*
> *—Tony Evans*

There is only one God, and he is unlike any other. In 1 Kings 18, we read about a great showdown between the prophets of a pretend god, named Baal, and Elijah, the prophet of the one true God.

On Mount Carmel, Elijah issued a great challenge: Both he and the false prophets would build grand altars and then kill a bull to offer as a sacrifice on the altar. However, neither Elijah nor the prophets of Baal would light their offering on fire. Instead, they'd call upon their gods to light up the offering by sending fire from heaven.

The prophets of Baal went first. They prepared an offering and prayed to their gods for an entire morning. By noon, Elijah began to taunt and make fun of them: "Shout louder!" he said. "Your god must be deep in thought, or busy, or traveling, or in the bathroom! Maybe he's asleep and you need to wake him up!"

When Elijah had enough, he and his helper poured barrels of water on their altar; they made it so that it would be even more difficult to light. Then, Elijah prayed to God, the one true God . . . and he answered. Boy did he answer! God sent fire from heaven that burned up the offering, the stones of the altar, and even some of the ground underneath.

God showed the people that he is the only God, greater than anything else they were tempted to love or worship. God alone is our almighty Creator, our standard of love, goodness, perfection, knowledge, and truth. No one is like him! That's why in God's law we are instructed not to let anything else come close to the kind of love and honor we give to God.

Not our families, or our favorite video games, or our Lego creations. Nothing we can love is as great as God. Even though we might show great devotion to our favorite things, they make bad gods. They can't answer our prayers, and they won't satisfy our deepest needs. There is only one God. He alone is worthy of our worship, honor, and praise.

THINK ABOUT IT

• What are you tempted to love and honor more than God?

>>> **PRAY:** *God, you alone are God, but we fail to love you best. Thank you for being faithful to us even when we are not faithful to you. Amen.*

In how many persons does God exist?

Three. God the Father, God the Son, and God the Holy Spirit.

MEMORY VERSE:
May the grace of the Lord Jesus Christ, and the love of God, and fellowship of the Holy Spirit be with you all. 2 Corinthians 13:14

Power-up Question:
What is your favorite thing that comes in a set of three?

>>> READ JOHN 17:20-24

Being triune, God is a sharing God, a God who loves to include. Indeed, that is why God creates. His love is not for keeping but for spreading.
—Michael Reeves

In the last devotional, we learned there is only one true God. But the Bible also teaches us that the one true God exists in three persons—God the Father, God the Son, and God the Holy Spirit. You can find the three persons in many places in the Bible—at Creation and in the Great Commission's command to baptize in the name of the Father, the Son, and the Holy Spirit as well. Another clear place is the very last verse of Paul's second letter to the Corinthians. 2 Corinthians 13:14 says, "May the grace of the Lord Jesus Christ [the Son], and the love of God [the Father], and the fellowship of the Holy Spirit be with you all."

The truth of one God in three persons stretches our brains. You've probably learned from math class that $1 + 1 + 1 = 3$. So, how can three persons be one God? Our belief that God is three—what Christians for centuries have called the doctrine of the Trinity—isn't just a weird math problem. It's terribly important.

Have you ever thought about what God was doing before he made you, and me, and the world? Do you know that the Bible tells us? In John 17:24, Jesus prays, "Father . . . you loved me before the creation of the world." Before God the Father did anything else . . . Before he created the world, formed Adam and Eve, and called Abraham . . . Before he rescued Israel from Egypt or made David king . . . from all eternity, God the Father was *loving* the Son.

You see, if God were just one person, he would have no one to love. But from all eternity, God the Father has been loving Jesus. And not just that. When two people are in love, they'll pair up, and they can be sort of, well, exclusive.

But God the Father didn't just share his love by being Father to God the Son. The Father and Son, from all eternity, have shared their love with the Spirit, too. The Trinity shows us that God isn't greedy, ungenerous, or cliquish with his love. God *is* love through and through. And because God *is* love, he doesn't keep his love to himself. God loves to share.

THINK ABOUT IT

• What's the difference between God the Creator and a video game designer?

• Would it be silly if we asked a game designer to love and give himself for his characters? Why?

>>> PRAY: *God, we're so thankful for your great love. Thank you, Father, for demonstrating your love to us by sending the Son. Thank you, Father and Son, for pouring out your love into our hearts by the Holy Spirit. Amen.*

Is God great?

Yes, and his greatness cannot be measured.

Is God good?

Yes. No one is truly good except God.

MEMORY VERSE:
Great is the Lᴏʀᴅ and most worthy of praise; his greatness no one can fathom . . . The Lᴏʀᴅ is good to all; he has compassion on all he has made.
Psalm 145:3, 9

Power-up Question:
What is your favorite water-themed world or level in a video game?

>>> READ PSALM 145

 To write the love of God above would drain the ocean dry; nor could the scroll contain the whole, though stretched from sky to sky.
—Frederick Martin Lehman , "The Love of God"

Psalm 145:3 says, "Great is the Lord and most worthy of praise; his greatness no one can fathom." The last word, *fathom*, is a difficult one. What does it mean?

If you hear someone today say, "I can't fathom that," they probably mean something like, "That's really hard to understand." But in Bible times, the word had a different meaning. In ancient times, sailors would use something called a sounding line to measure the depth of the ocean.

By *a sounding line*, we don't mean that it made a sound, except maybe *plop*! A sounding line was a length of rope with a piece of lead attached to the end. The lead would make the rope sink down to the bottom of the water. However far the rope sank, that's how many fathoms deep the water was.

In the old days, most sounding lines measured up to one hundred fathoms. With that tool, a sailor could measure any ocean depth close to shore. But when he sailed out to sea, there came a point when the waters were out of sounding. They were too deep to be measured.

Psalm 145:3 tells us God can't be fathomed. It's saying he's too big to measure. People can understand God truly, but we can't understand him completely, because God is deeper than the ocean. We can't measure God with hours or minutes because God is timeless and eternal. We can't measure God with miles or inches because God is everywhere; he fills all things. We can't measure God's strength with pounds or tons because God is omnipotent; he is all-powerful.

And God isn't just great without measure. He's also thoroughly good. He's wise, holy, just, loving, and true. God is perfect and undivided in all of his attributes. He's perfectly great, and he's fully good. And that's why we praise him!

THINK ABOUT IT

• Think of three reasons why God is worthy of your praise. Take time to praise him right now.

>>> PRAY: *God, thank you for being the great God. You are unchangeable, eternal, all powerful, and ever present. Thank you for being the good God. You are wise, holy, loving, just, and true. Thank you for showing us your goodness and greatness in Jesus. Amen.*

Why did God make you?

God made us to enjoy him and
show his glory to others.

What is God's glory?

God's glory is his goodness and
greatness shining out to the world.

MEMORY VERSE:
For the earth will be filled with the knowledge
of the glory of the LORD as the waters cover the sea.
Habakkuk 2:14

Power-up Question:
What do you enjoy about playing
video games?

>>> **READ PSALM 19**

> *What is the chief end of man? To glorify God and enjoy him forever.*
> —*Westminster Shorter Catechism*

The Bible doesn't give us a simplistic definition of God's glory. Instead, it shows us examples. We see God's glory in the way he creates, how God speaks about himself, demonstrates his power, and how he loves and cares for his people. God's glory isn't just one of his characteristics—like his unsearchable knowledge, all-powerful strength, or perfect love. Instead, it's every aspect of God's goodness and perfection shining out for the world to see.

God wired us to long for and seek after glorious things. We're drawn to glory when we wake up to six inches of beautiful, fluffy snow. Even if we don't recognize God's creative hand behind the snow, we're in awe of it, and we want to play in it. We also experience God's glory when we taste incredible food—like stuffed crust pizza! Do you realize that God created our tiny taste buds and the laws of science that help that crust get perfectly crispy? Stuffed crust is just one of the small things that puts God's glory on display!

We're also drawn to the stories of glory in the Bible, and we learn that God made us to display his glory. He wants us to live in loving relationship with him and others, and he wants us to steward his creation as bearers of his image.

In 2013, the video game brand EA Sports stopped making its college football and basketball games because the company had gotten in trouble. Why? They were using pictures and images in their games that looked like real college players, but they weren't giving those athletes any of the money they made from selling the games.

Because we're made in God's image, he wants us to give him the glory he is due. Just like the sports video games carried the "image and likeness" of many college athletes, we carry God's image and likeness. As a result, we owe him honor and praise in return.

Sometimes, we want to keep glory for ourselves instead of giving honor to God. But when our hearts turn toward Jesus, we can give thanks for the beauty his hands have made. We see God at work in our lives as we walk through times of joy and suffering, and we thank God for his presence with us. Best of all, when we experience God's glory, we share that joy and excitement with everyone around us.

THINK ABOUT IT

• What does your obedience or disobedience reveal about your love for Christ? Does it magnify or diminish his name and image in the eyes of others?

>>> PRAY: God, you are wonderful and glorious! Help us to show your goodness and greatness in the way we trust and obey you.

How did God form the first man?

God formed Adam from the dust.

How did God form the first woman?

God formed the woman from the man.

MEMORY VERSE:
Then the LORD God formed a man from the dust of the ground and breathed into his nostrils the breath of life, and the man became a living being . . . Then the LORD God made a woman from the rib he had taken out of the man, and he brought her to the man. Genesis 2:7, 22

Power-up Question:
What have you created that you're proud of?

>>> READ GENESIS 1:26-27 AND 2:4-25

God invested their bodies with strengths and weaknesses that would bind them together in mutual dependence . . . Together they would rule and reign over the new creation as King and Queen.
—Wendy Alsup and Hannah Anderson

It's important for us to understand how and why God created Adam and Eve, because that's where we came from. Everyone's family tree traces back to them, and God has given us the same gifts of life and humanity that he gave to them at creation.

Today's question has us consider the creation of Adam and Eve—how God made man from the dust (Genesis 2:7), and the woman from Adam's rib (v. 22).

Genesis 1:26–27 tells us that God created people in his image and likeness. This means that the way people live, think, and relate to one another reflects God's life, reason, and heart. God gave people a mind to think, create, and solve problems. He gave us hearts to experience joy, love, excitement, sadness, and hope.

God also made a distinction between men and women. Both men and women are equally made in the image of God, but they are different from one another. He made them male and female. God said it wasn't good for Adam to be alone (Genesis 2:18), so he made a mate for him. God didn't make a copy of Adam; he created someone new and different to complement him.

The word *complement* (with an *e* in the middle) doesn't mean to say nice things about someone (that's *compliment* with an *i*). No, God made the woman to *complete* the man. Eve was strong in ways Adam was weak, and the same was true of Adam for Eve. Like two characters in a video game, men and women play off one another's strengths.

God didn't create the man and woman to stare at each other and twiddle their thumbs. God gave them something to do. He made them to live and work together in the world he made. He made them both in his image to watch over his world. Just as God rules and reigns over the world, he's called humanity to rule and cultivate the earth—to grow crops, make families, and build cities. He's called us to world-build. We started with a little dust and a rib bone, and now we carry a lot of responsibility.

THINK ABOUT IT

• What gifts has God given you that complement your family?

>>> **PRAY:** *Father, we thank you for the gift of life. Who are we that you're so mindful of us—creating us in your image? Thank you for giving us everything we need. Amen.*

How do we show God's glory?

We show God's glory by loving, trusting, and obeying him.

MEMORY VERSE:
So whether you eat or drink or whatever you do, do it all for the glory of God.
1 Corinthians 10:31

Power-up Question:
What's your favorite co-op game where you had to work together to win?

>>> READ 1 CORINTHIANS 10:23-33

❝❝ *The glory of God is a human being fully alive. —Irenaeus*

You might remember that God's glory isn't one of his characteristics, but instead it's all his perfections shining forth for all to see. God's glory displays everything good and true about him!

But why does God involve us in displaying his glory? Why has he made us as people who bear his image—who wear his name? Imagine for a moment that it's a Saturday afternoon in May and you're heading out to the ballpark. Your favorite team is the Louisville Bats, and their star third baseman (and power hitter!) is the great Mighty Casey. On the way to the game, you hear on the radio that Casey has been traded to the opposing team—the Mudville Nine!

Before Casey was traded, he wore the words *Louisville Bats* on his jersey. The logo with the letters *B-A-T-S* was written there across the front in that beautiful red, navy, and white. He had the bat logo on his cap. He practiced with the Louisville team, and you could see his name in the lineup on the scoreboard. But now Casey has been traded and he bears a different name.

It's sad when our favorite player is traded. They aren't repping the colors and name *and glory* of your favorite team anymore. In a similar way, God wants our whole lives to revolve around his glory. He doesn't simply want us to wear shirts and caps with Jesus's name or Bible verses on them—though that's okay. More importantly, he wants us to spend time with him so the truth we learn in his Word shapes our thinking. He wants our hearts and affections to turn toward him. He wants us to love him and trust him.

Sometimes we want to keep glory for ourselves instead of giving glory and honor to God. But as we turn our hearts toward Jesus, we can praise him for his faithful presence in our lives—through joy and suffering. As we trust his Word and obey his commands, we share our love for God with others.

THINK ABOUT IT

• First Peter 4:16 says, "If you suffer as a Christian, do not be ashamed, but praise God that you bear that name." What does it mean to bear the name of Christ?

>>> **PRAY:** *God, you are wonderful and glorious! Help us to show your goodness and greatness in the way we trust and obey you. Amen.*

Where do we learn to love, trust, and obey God?

In the Bible.

Can we trust the Bible?

Yes. The Bible is completely true and without any mistakes.

MEMORY VERSE:
All Scripture is God-breathed and is useful for teaching, rebuking, correcting and training in righteousness. 2 Timothy 3:16

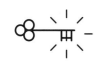

Power-up Question:
If you were a video game writer, what story would you tell?

>>> READ 2 TIMOTHY 3:16-17

 All other writing is to lead the way into and point toward the Scriptures, as John the Baptist did toward Christ. —Martin Luther

In our world—at least in the US—Bibles are everywhere. You might find more than one on a bookshelf in your home. You can find the Bible in lots of versions on the internet. And you can even download a Bible app for your tablet or phone.

The Bible is everywhere, but sometimes we take it for granted. We're tempted to think that it's only something we take to church with us on Sundays. But God wants us to spend time reading our Bibles every day. The Bible is God's holy Word. Even though it was written by human authors, those men were taught by the Holy Spirit. So, now, when we read the words of Moses or David or Matthew or Paul, we're also reading God's very words—his personal letter to you and me.

The Bible teaches us, warns us when we're off track, and helps us get back on the right one. In this way, the Bible shows us how to love, trust, and obey God. We use the Bible the same way game avatars might use a lantern in front of their feet to light their path. Just like a flashlight, the Bible shows us where to go.

The Bible is *true* and *trustworthy*. God doesn't lie, so we can count on his words. Because the Bible is true, it's also our *authority*—our rule for living. The Bible is also *clear*. While some of the things we find in the 66 books of the Bible—like in Revelation or Ezekiel or Leviticus—are difficult to understand, the Bible's main point and central message make sense. And that's important because the Bible is also *necessary*. We *need* God's clear words for us to understand how to live. It's like bread to feed our hungry souls. We can't live without it.

The Bible is true, clear, authoritative, and necessary. The most important thing about the Bible, though, is that it *teaches us about Jesus*. The religious leaders in Jesus's day loved the Scriptures, but they saw their Bible as a book of religious rules and examples. Jesus said to them, "You study the Scriptures diligently because you think that in them you have eternal life. These are the very Scriptures that testify about me" (John 5:39). You see, the ancient scribes and Pharisees (the know-it-all leaders of the Jewish people) missed the point. The Bible doesn't only tell us how to live. It points us to Jesus as our Savior.

THINK ABOUT IT

• Where do you often like to read God's Word? Is there a special place you like to go?

>>> PRAY: *Father, thank you for the gift of your Word, and for your Spirit that makes it clear to us as we read and study. Give us wisdom as we study your Word. Help us to move its truths from the pages of our Bibles into our own hearts. Amen.*

LEVEL 2

GOD'S KINGDOM

2-10 2-11
2-12
2-13
2-1
2-14

What is God's kingdom?

Where we live life with God under his loving rule.

MEMORY VERSE:
The kingdom of heaven is like treasure hidden in a field. When a man found it, he hid it again, and then in his joy went and sold all he had and bought that field. Matthew 13:44

Power-up Question:
What's your favorite fictional kingdom?

>>> READ MATTHEW 13:44-46

> " For Jesus, the word "kingdom" meant "God's dream for this world come true." —Scot McKnight

God's kingdom is where we live life with God under his loving rule. God's kingdom is the place where God's dream for the world comes true.

When you hear the words *king* or *queen*, what do you think about? Do you think of a king from a cartoon like Sleeping Beauty—someone who might be kind-hearted but cowers in the face of an enemy? Do you think of an evil emperor—like Bowser in the mushroom kingdom—who makes all his people live in fear? Do you think of a good and strong king like the Black Panther whose rule is just and good, but whose kingdom is always under threat of attack, one where in every new adventure, there are new rivals for the throne?

God made the whole world and everything in it. And because God made the world, he's in charge of the world. God rules over everything. He is the king! But God's rule isn't weak, selfish, or threatened like that of human kings. God is good, just, loving, powerful, and eternal! His kingdom is truly the best kingdom.

The Bible tells us that it's worth giving our whole life to be a part of his kingdom. Like the man who found the treasure in the field or the merchant who saw the pearl at the market, when you find God's kingdom, you know that it's worth sacrificing everything to be a part of it!

IT'S WORTH GIVING OUR WHOLE LIFE TO BE PART OF HIS KINGDOM.

THINK ABOUT IT

- What makes God's kingdom the most beautiful and best?
- What do we have to give up to gain the wonders of God's kingdom?

>>> **PRAY:** *Jesus, thank you for sacrificing your life for our lives. For the joy set before you—for the joy of life in the kingdom with us—you endured the sufferings of the cross. Help us to see the wonderful joy of living forever under your rule in your kingdom. Amen.*

How does God command us to live in his kingdom?

We are commanded to love God and our neighbor.

How should we love God?

We love God by obeying and serving only him.

How does God tell us to love our neighbor?

We should love our neighbor as ourselves.

MEMORY VERSE: Jesus replied, "'Love the Lord your God with all your heart and with all your soul and with all your mind.' This is the first and greatest commandment. And the second is like it: 'Love your neighbor as yourself.' All the Law and the Prophets hang on these two commandments." Matthew 22:37–40

Power-up Question:
Do you find in-game tutorials helpful, or would you rather figure out a game on your own? Why or why not?

>>> READ MATTHEW 22:34-40

> *The law doesn't just show us our sin so we might be drawn to Christ; it shows us how to live as those who belong to Christ.* —Kevin DeYoung

A Pharisee asked Jesus, "Which of the commandments is the greatest?" Jesus's answer points us to two passages in the Old Testament: Deuteronomy 6:5 and Leviticus 19:18. If someone goes through the trouble of repeating something old, it's probably important. That's what Jesus does here. We should listen to his words!

Jesus instructs us to love God with everything we have, with our entire heart, soul, and mind. We put following Jesus before everything else—baseball, video games, sleepovers, and our favorite TV show. Those other things aren't bad, but we must seek God before we chase after anything else. He must get our best, not our leftovers.

Jesus wants us to love God by obeying and serving only him. This isn't a commandment we should take lightly, and it isn't something that's optional for Christ-followers. But how do we love God and find ways to serve him? Often, we love God by loving others.

Jesus tells us that we must love our neighbors as ourselves. He wants us to treat the people in our lives—our families, friends, and those who live around us—the same way we'd want to be treated. In the same way we take good care of ourselves, we do the same for our neighbors. We must be kind, generous, honest, and helpful.

Sometimes God invites us to love him and others by doing difficult things—like traveling around the world to tell people about Jesus. Other times his commands are simple but no less important—like being a good listener. As we read and study God's Word, pray and grow in our love and affection for God and others, we grow in our skill and ability to live as his kingdom-people.

THINK ABOUT IT

• What are some specific ways you can express your love for God?
• What are some ways you and your family can love your neighbors?

>>> PRAY: *Father, thank you for demonstrating your love for us by sending your Son, Jesus, to die on our behalf and invite us back to life with you. Help us to grow in our love for you, and for our neighbors. Amen.*

Why does God tell us, "You shall have no other gods before me"?

Because God is our only King and Lord.

Why does God tell us, "You shall not make for yourself an image"?

So we will serve God and nothing else.

MEMORY VERSE:
You shall have no other gods before me. You shall not make for yourself an image . . .You shall not misuse the name of the LORD your God . . . Remember the Sabbath day by keeping it holy. Exodus 20:3–8, abbreviated

Power-up Question:
When have you gotten into big trouble?
How can gaming get someone into trouble?

>>> READ EXODUS 20:1–6 AND 32:1–35

God had delivered his people from slavery in Egypt by sending plagues against the Egyptians and then drowning Pharaoh and his army in the Red Sea. After crossing through the sea, Moses led the people to Mount Sinai. He climbed up the mountain and spoke to God for several days.

While he was on the mountain, God gave Moses his law and commandments on stone tablets, and the first two commandments were: (1) You shall have no other gods before me, and (2) You shall not make for yourself an image of a bird or an animal.

But Moses stayed up on the mountain for a long time. He stayed so long, the people grew impatient. They thought Moses wasn't coming back. So, the people went to Moses's brother Aaron and said, "Make us gods who will lead us." Aaron replied, "Give me all of your gold earrings, necklaces, coins, and chains." Then, Aaron melted the gold in a fire and shaped it into a baby cow—a golden calf.

After Aaron and the people crafted their false god, they threw a party! They danced, praised, and worshiped the golden calf saying, "This is our god who saved us from Egypt!" Uh-oh! The people had broken God's first two commands.

Moses hurried down the mountain with the two stone tablets. When he saw what the people were doing, he was angry. He threw the stone tablets to the ground and they broke into pieces. Then, he ground up the golden calf into powder, mixed it with water, and made the people drink it. Moses said to Aaron, "What have you done?" And Aaron told a big, fat lie: "The people gave me the gold. I threw it into the fire. Then this cow popped out!"

God's law teaches us to worship only him. It teaches us to respect, love, and trust God above all things. But very often we trust other things instead of God. We want to follow our own way instead of God's way, and then we'll even lie to cover it up.

Moses was sad, but instead of growing in anger toward Aaron and others, he prayed. He said, "God, don't forget about your promises. Please forgive the people's sin."

THINK ABOUT IT

• What happens when you get in trouble? Are you able to tell anyone? Who can you ask for prayer?

>>> **PRAY:** *Jesus, even when we sin—even when we break your very first command—you still love us. Thank you for praying for us and offering your forgiveness. Amen.*

Why does God tell us, "You shall not misuse the name of the Lᴏʀᴅ your God"?

So we will honor and respect God's name and character.

MEMORY VERSE:
Ascribe to the Lᴏʀᴅ, you heavenly beings,
ascribe to the Lᴏʀᴅ glory and strength.
Ascribe to the Lᴏʀᴅ the glory due his name;
worship the Lᴏʀᴅ in the splendor of his holiness.
Psalm 29:1–2

Power-up Question:
Tell about a time gaming brought the worst out of you. How were others affected?

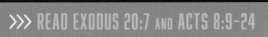

>>> READ EXODUS 20:7 ᴀɴᴅ ACTS 8:9–24

The Bible tells us that God's name should be honored because it reflects his character. Many people think this commandment is just about using God's name as a swear word, so they avoid shouting, "Christ!" when they stub their toe, or texting, "OMG!" to their friends. That's certainly part of it. But God also commands that we have the self-control to honor him with our words.

God's third commandment is about more than cursing. He also forbids his people from using his name in careless and wicked ways. In Leviticus, we see that people in Bible times were punished and killed for cursing God's name (24:16).

Leviticus also tells people not to swear empty oaths (19:12). That means you shouldn't make a promise if you don't mean it. The kid who says, "I swear to God" but keeps his fingers crossed, is breaking the third commandment. And the adult who puts their hand on a Bible in court and swears to tell the truth but then lies anyway has broken this command, too.

Another way to break the third commandment is by being a false prophet or a sorcerer. There are wizards like Gandalf and Dumbledore in good stories. But the Bible warns us specifically about false prophets and teachers like Simon the Magician who say they are following God but are actually seeking to do supernatural things to serve themselves (Ezekiel 13:21–22; Acts 8:9–24). In a similar way, if you try to use God's name as a magic word to make your wishes come true, you're also breaking the third commandment.

But even if we aren't using Jesus's name as a swear word, to predict the future, or cast spells, this commandment is still important to us. The Bible doesn't only tell us what not to do with God's name; it also tells how to honor God's name. God wants us to speak the truth and pray in his *name*, saying words that show honor both to God and our neighbors.

THINK ABOUT IT

• How are you tempted to misuse God's name?

>>> **PRAY:** *Lord, help us to live lives that honor your great name. Amen.*

Why does God tell us, "Remember the Sabbath day by keeping it holy"?

So we will rest in God and remember the finished work of Jesus.

MEMORY VERSE:

Remember the Sabbath day by keeping it holy. Six days you shall labor and do all your work, but the seventh day is a sabbath to the LORD your God . . . For in six days the LORD made the heavens and the earth, the sea, and all that is in them, but he rested on the seventh day. Exodus 20:8–11a

Power-up Question:
What video games help you relax? How?

>>> READ EXODUS 20:8-11
AND DEUTERONOMY 15:12-15

It's humans who recognize the difference between work and rest. The fact that we make distinctions . . . is an indication we need to do both.
—Adele Calhoun

Have you ever been attacked by the Minecraft phantom? In the video game *Minecraft*, each player must go back to his bed every so often to rest. Don't get distracted by building high mountain bases and skyscrapers, or by digging deep into the game's cavernous depths. If you do, and you forget to sleep, a mob of enemies will come after you at night!

Making your Minecraft avatar need sleep was a brilliant choice by the game's designers. After all, we all need rest! If we never stop and get some sleep, we stop functioning well, and we'll eventually go crazy and die.

But rest isn't only an essential for life, it's God's instruction to his people in the fourth commandment. God is more thorough than the Minecraft designers. He doesn't stop at telling his people to sleep at night, he tells them to set aside an entire day for Sabbath. There are two big reasons why: God wanted Israel to stop each week to remember both his rest and their rescue.

First, Exodus 20:8–11 tells us one reason we should set aside a day of rest—because God rested on the seventh day. God doesn't need to rest. He doesn't get tired or wear out as we do, but God paused his creation work as an example for us. He made us for Sabbath because he wants us to stop, follow his pattern, and remember we are creatures who depend on him (Psalm 127:2).

Second, in Deuteronomy 5:12–15, God emphasizes the need for the whole Israelite community to rest: "that your male and female servants may rest, as you do" (v. 14). There's no class distinction because everyone in the community was once a slave. On the Sabbath, all Israel set aside a day to worship and remember how he'd rescued the nation. They did not save themselves. No, God brought the community out of Egypt through a great display of his might and power.

As Christians, we too set aside a day for worship and renewal. From the earliest days of the church, Jesus's disciples met together on the first day of the week. Sunday was the day Jesus was raised from the dead. So, every Lord's Day we remember and celebrate our salvation.

THINK ABOUT IT

• What do you like about going to church?

>>> PRAY: *Father, thank you for setting aside a day for our bodies, minds, and hearts to rest. Give us grace to pause life and remember that your work is finished! Amen.*

Why does God tell us, "Honor your father and mother"?

So we will love and obey our parents.

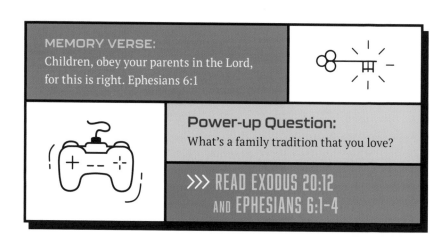

MEMORY VERSE:
Children, obey your parents in the Lord, for this is right. Ephesians 6:1

Power-up Question:
What's a family tradition that you love?

>>> READ EXODUS 20:12
AND EPHESIANS 6:1-4

> At the heart of the madness of the gospel is an almost unbelievable mystery . . . to be seen and known and loved by a father.
> —James K. A. Smith

My (Trey's) family got a Nintendo Switch recently and my kids and I have been playing a lot of *Mario Kart*. My son is a Karting master. He knows all the shortcuts, the places to drift around corners, and how to get secret boosts all along the track. When we get to the end of a race, we take a moment to congratulate the winner (usually him) as the trophy shows up on the screen. It's a moment to honor the champion before the trash talk starts again for the next race.

When God tells us to honor our father and mother (as well as our grandparents and guardians), he isn't telling us to wake up each day and offer medals to our parents. He wants us to honor them with the way we live. There are lots of ways to do that every day. We can listen carefully, speak kindly, and be thankful. But in Ephesians 6:1, Paul tells us that the primary way to honor our parents is to obey them.

Throughout the Old Testament, God pleads with his people to listen and obey. God knows what's best and he wants his people to follow him, so they'll experience happiness and blessing. But again and again God's people went their own way instead of following his plan. Despite their continued disobedience, God cared for his people. He always pursued them and at the right time, he sent his Son, Jesus, so they might be forgiven.

When we honor our father and mother, we show love to God, because he is also our Father. The bad news is that we will fail at this, just like the Israelites. We might forget what our parents tell us, or choose a path that rebels against them. But God offers us his forgiveness and grace even when we mess up. He offers us both forgiveness and strength to listen, obey, and show them love, kindness, and gratitude.

THINK ABOUT IT

• When is it difficult to follow instructions from your parents or others in your family? Parents, what can you say or do to make it easier for your kids to listen and obey?

>>> **PRAY:** *God, help us to trust you as our Good Father. And help us to show love, honor, and obedience to our parents, grandparents, and caregivers. Amen.*

Why does God tell us, "You shall not murder"?

So we will not hate or be hateful to others but rather love and befriend them.

MEMORY VERSE:
Then the Lord said to Cain, "Why are you angry? Why is your face downcast? If you do what is right, will you not be accepted? But if you do not do what is right, sin is crouching at your door; it desires to have you, but you must rule over it." Genesis 4:6–7

Power-up Question:
What frustrates you?
What really gets on your nerves?

>>> READ EXODUS 20:13 AND GENESIS 4

We should fear and love God so that we do not hurt or harm our neighbor in his body, but help and support him in every physical need.
—Martin Luther

Cain was a farmer, and Abel was a shepherd. Both brothers brought an offering to God. Cain brought some of his crops, but Abel brought choice cuts of meat from the firstborn of his flock. The Bible tells us God looked favorably upon Abel's offering but didn't accept what Cain brought (Hebrews 11:4; cf. 1 John 3:12). Cain didn't like that. He grew jealous of his brother and angry with God. That's when God warned him: "Why is your face downcast? If you do what is right, will you not be accepted?" (Genesis 4:6b–7a). Cain didn't heed God's warning. His jealousy and hatred grew. One day, while Cain and Abel were in a field, Cain murdered his brother.

There are a few things we can learn from this sad story:

First, *God wants us to guard our hearts*. The root of murder is jealousy, anger, and revenge—evil attitudes that begin within (Matthew 5:21–22).

Second, *God wants us to love and respect him*. Allowing anger against God to grow will ultimately lead us to harm others. It was Cain's cold and unbelieving heart toward God that got him in trouble in the first place.

Third, *we learn to love and not hate by remembering how God loved us*. Abel's blood cried out from the ground as a witness against Cain (Genesis 4:10). Cain's crops would no longer grow, and he was cursed to wander the earth. But when Cain cried out, "My punishment is more than I can bear" (v. 13), God showed him grace. He put a mark of protection on Cain so no one would harm him. God has shown even greater grace to us. Jesus spilled his blood for our jealous and hateful hearts. Hebrews tells us that his blood "speaks a better word than the blood of Abel" (12:24). Instead of being a witness *against* us, Jesus's blood testifies *for* our salvation.

THINK ABOUT IT

• Do you feel any anger or jealousy in your heart? Confess it. Pray that God's Holy Spirit will help you to love others.

>>> **PRAY:** *Father, equip us to treat all people with kindness and love. Amen.*

Why does God tell us, "You shall not steal"?

So we will not take what belongs to others but instead desire to give.

MEMORY VERSE:
Do not defraud or rob your neighbor.
Do not hold back the wages of a hired worker overnight. Leviticus 19:13

Power-up Question:
When have you experienced someone's generosity toward you?

>>> READ EXODUS 20:15 AND LUKE 19:1-10

It is beyond the realm of possibilities that one has the ability to out give God. Even if I give the whole of my worth to him, he will find a way to give back to me much more than I gave. —Charles Spurgeon

In the *Legend of Zelda: Link's Awakening*, stealing isn't taken lightly. In the game's village, there's a town tool shop where players can buy items they need to help them along their journey. If you steal items from the store instead of paying for them, there are consequences. Everyone in the village calls you "Thief!" for the rest of the game. And if you dare to reenter the tool shop, its owner will cause you to immediately lose the game.

Zacchaeus could relate to being called a thief. He was chief tax collector in Jericho. The Roman empire taxed the people of that city, and it was Zacchaeus's job to collect the payments. Like many tax collectors, Zacchaeus was dishonest. He charged people more than they owed, and he kept the extra money for himself. Zacchaeus was stealing, breaking the eighth commandment. He abused his position to cheat the people and take what didn't belong to him. For this reason, the people of Jericho despised Zacchaeus.

All that changed when Zacchaeus met Jesus. When Jesus came to Jericho, Zacchaeus climbed a tree to get a better view. As Jesus walked by, he looked up and said, "Zacchaeus, come down immediately. I must stay at your house today." The crowds wondered why Jesus would want to spend time with a crooked thief, but Zacchaeus's heart was filled with joy. He was changed completely! Zacchaeus said, "Look, Lord! Here and now I give half of my possessions to the poor." The tax collector abandoned his thievery and gave back all he stole and more.

Jesus wants to change us. The Bible says, "Anyone who has been stealing must steal no longer, but must work, doing something useful with their own hands, that they may have something to share with those in need" (Ephesians 4:28). Jesus wants to take greedy, selfish hearts and make them generous toward others.

THINK ABOUT IT

• How can you be generous to others this week?

>>> **PRAY:** *Father, help us to be happy with what you've given us and generous to those who have need.*

Why does God tell us, "You shall not give false testimony against your neighbor"?

So we will tell the truth as God does and not speak evil of one another.

MEMORY VERSE:
The Lord detests lying lips, but he delights in people who are trustworthy. Proverbs 12:22

Power-up Question:
Tell about a time you were tempted to lie. What happened?

>>> READ EXODUS 20:16
AND COLOSSIANS 3:9-10

> *Lies! Deceptions! Every day more lies!*
> —*Saw Gerrera,* Rogue One: A Star Wars Story

To me (Kevin), the Justice League is one of the greatest superhero teams. They're a diverse group—cyborgs, humans, Atlanteans, Amazonians, and Guardians from the sky. Together, they unite in the name of justice to protect the world from those who would seek to harm and destroy the innocent.

But it isn't just superheroes who fight for what is right. God has been working long before this comic book and video game team-up. He protects the innocent and ensures that evil people pay for their wrongs. When God established his law, he created a system that was good, fair, and right. When he commanded his people not to give false testimony against their neighbor, he wanted the wicked to stop spreading lies about others for selfish gain. He also wanted to protect the innocent from being punished for crimes they didn't commit (Zechariah 8:16).

There are many reasons we may be tempted to lie about our neighbors. Have you ever done something you knew you weren't supposed to do? To get out of trouble, were you tempted to blame your friend, or your sibling? Have you ever been tempted to lie about someone to repay a wrong done to you?

When we choose to tell lies instead of the truth, we're choosing to harm others instead of loving them. Though it may seem harmless, spreading lies at the expense of someone else isn't right. It's unjust, because lying always has a cost. It can damage a neighbor's reputation, stir them up with anger, or bring them great pain and shame.

When we choose to tell lies, we're also sinning against God. God loves the truth and hates lies. The Bible says that it's impossible for God to lie (Hebrews 6:18). When we lie, we're acting against the very character and nature of God. Instead, we're following after the father of lies, Satan himself (John 8:44). But when we speak the truth, we give God glory and reflect God's justice and love.

THINK ABOUT IT

• Take turns sharing an encouraging truth about another family member.

>>> **PRAY:** *Father, help us to reflect your character by speaking the truth to one another and putting away all falsehood. Amen.*

Why does God tell us, "You shall not covet"?

So we will be content with what we have.

Why does God tell us, "You shall not commit adultery"?

So we will live pure and faithful lives, abstaining from sexual immorality, whether we are married or single.

MEMORY VERSE:
Blessed are the pure in heart, for they will see God.
Matthew 5:8

Power-up Question:
When have you waited a long time for something? Take turns sharing together.

>>> READ EXODUS 20:14, 17
AND 2 SAMUEL 11–12

 We're sinners. The precise details of our sin may not correspond with David's, but the presence and recurrence of sin does.
—Eugene Peterson

King David was Israel's most beloved king. He was a man after God's own heart (1 Samuel 13:14), but he did not always follow God's will. One spring when Israel's army went off to war, David stayed home at the palace. One evening, he went up to his balcony roof and saw a woman bathing. David thought she was beautiful, so he asked his servants to find out who she was. The servants told David that the woman's name was Bathsheba and that she was married to one of his generals, Uriah. David still wanted Bathsheba. So, he sent his servants to take her. David broke the tenth commandment, "You shall not covet."

We covet when we want something that does not belong to us. There's nothing wrong with wanting good things. Maybe you want a new bike or video game. When young people are growing up, they sometimes want to get a certain job or to get married. These can be good desires. But it's a problem when our desires become all we can think about and we refuse to be satisfied until we get what we want.

Coveting is a sin that begins in our heart, but it often opens the door to other sinful actions, like stealing or greedy hoarding of money. David wanted Bathsheba so much that he disobeyed God's command, "You shall not commit adultery." Adultery occurs when a married person is unfaithful to their spouse. David was a married man, but he acted like he was married to a woman, Bathsheba, who was not his wife. And David's bad behavior didn't stop there. David's coveting led to him lying about his sin and then committing murder to conceal it.

God wants us to be content. He wants us to have pure hearts that are happy and satisfied with what we have, not sinfully wanting more. The secret to being content is not putting our hope in what we want, but instead putting our hope in God who loves us and takes care of us whatever our circumstances (Philippians 4:11–13).

THINK ABOUT IT

• Are there desires in your heart that have grown into covetousness? Confess these desires to a family member and ask them to pray for you.

>>> **PRAY:** *Father, help us to learn the secret of being content. Help us to remember that you love us and will always take care of us. Help us to rely on your strength. Amen.*

Who can obey God's law?

No one but Jesus can obey God's law perfectly.

If no one can obey God's law, why did God give it?

God gave the law to show us
his goodness, to show us our sin,
and to show us we need Jesus.

MEMORY VERSE:
"You study the Scriptures diligently because you think
that in them you have eternal life. These are the very
Scriptures that testify about me." John 5:39

Power-up Question:
Who is the toughest boss you've ever
defeated in a video game?

>>> READ ROMANS 3:9-24

> *A rigid master was the law, demanding brick, denying straw:*
> *But when with gospel-tongue it sings, it bids me fly, and gives me wings.*
> —Ralph Erskine

Paul gives us a clear picture of what the law was meant to do. It shows us God's goodness and perfection, but it also exposes our sin. When God reveals what he demands from us, we see the beauty of his plan. We want to pursue his perfect justice and love. But the law also reminds us that on our own, that pursuit is impossible.

Paul writes in Romans 3:23, "For all have sinned and fall short of the glory of God." He makes clear that no one—not even the best rule followers—can obey God's law perfectly. In verse 20 he tells us, "Therefore no one will be declared righteous in God's sight by the works of the law; rather, through the law we become conscious of our sin." So, is God with his law like a brutal video game boss that holds us in an endless loop of trying and failing, time and time again?

Of course not! Because he knew we couldn't keep his law, God sent his Son to keep the law perfectly for us. Jesus was tempted in every way we are, but he followed every command and remained completely free from sin (Hebrews 4:15). God's big-boss demand of perfect obedience didn't stand a chance against his own perfect Son. He is the Savior we need. If we ever forget this truth, the law faithfully reminds us of our sin and our great need for Jesus.

So, if righteousness doesn't come from keeping the law, can we still look to it for instruction? Yes. If you have a desire to follow God's commands, that's a good indicator that the Spirit is at work in your heart. We honor Christ and fulfill the law when we love God and others, but we never look to the law for our righteousness and salvation. That's forever secure through Jesus's life, death, and resurrection.

THINK ABOUT IT

- How does it feel knowing Jesus was tempted as we are?
- In what areas do you find it difficult to follow God's law? Ask the perfect Savior to give you victory.

>>> **PRAY:** *Father, thank you for the gift of your law. Give us the desire and strength to follow you as we rest in Jesus's perfect obedience for our salvation. Amen.*

What is sin?

Sin is saying "No" to God and doing what
we want instead of what God wants.

What happens because
of sin?

All people are lost and separated from
God because of our sin.

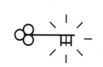

MEMORY VERSE:
For whoever keeps the whole law and yet
stumbles at just one point is guilty of breaking
all of it. James 2:10

Power-up Question:
If you could design your dream home,
what would it look like?

>>> READ GENESIS 3

> Sin and the child of God are incompatible. They may occasionally
> meet; they cannot live together in harmony. —John R. W. Stott

After God created people, he planted a garden for them in a land called Eden. The garden was beautiful! It had a sparkling river, the greenest plants, and trees that produced all sorts of delicious fruits. God was there, and he daily walked with the man and woman. He commanded Adam, "'You are free to eat from any tree in the garden; but you must not eat from the tree of the knowledge of good and evil, for when you eat from it you will certainly die'" (Genesis 2:16–17).

It sounds simple. Perfect place to live. All the food you can eat . . . except for one tree.

But when we turn the page to Genesis 3, everything falls apart. Satan enters the garden and tempts the woman to eat from the forbidden tree. Then, Adam follows and falls into sin as well.

The Bible tells us that because of our first parents' sin, everyone is born a sinner (Romans 5:13–14). Have you ever been upset with your parents? Lashed out at a brother or sister? Felt bitter towards a classmate? We commit sin because we have a sinful nature.

Sin twists who we are, and it affects what we do, say, think, and feel. Because of sin, we're lost and broken. We experience pain, suffering, guilt, shame, and death. Because of sin, our relationships are broken. We mistreat and hurt one another. Because of sin, all creation is broken. There are earthquakes, tornados, and diseases. Saddest of all, because of sin, our relationship with God was broken. All people are born separated from him, and because we sin, we deserve his punishment.

But we are not without hope. Amid the Genesis 3 story where it seems like everything has fallen apart, we find a glimmer of hope—a promise. God promises to send a rescuer, Jesus, who will defeat sin, death, and Satan once for all.

THINK ABOUT IT

- Where have you committed sin—on the playground, in the classroom, in your home, or in your heart? Confess it to God. Remember his promise: If we confess our sins, our loving God is faithful and just to forgive us (1 John 1:9).

>>> **PRAY:** God, we confess that we are sinful people. Please forgive us for the ways we've hurt each other and ourselves. Amen.

What does God demand from sinners before they can enter his kingdom?

We must turn from sin and have faith in Jesus.

—— ○ ——

MEMORY VERSE:
"The time has come," he said. "The kingdom of God has come near. Repent and believe the good news!" Mark 1:15

Power-up Question:
What's the longest video game quest you've ever embarked upon?

>>> READ MATTHEW 3:1-12

> *Our Lord and Master Jesus Christ willed the entire life of believers to be one of repentance. —Martin Luther*

Video game quests involve many twists and turns. Often you begin by talking with a wise old sage who gives you information for your journey. Then, you travel across the world to find a key. Once you find it, you turn around and again journey across the world to find a treasure chest. Once you open it and discover an ancient sword, you'll turn around again. This time, you're headed off to find a great wizard . . . So it goes in a video game quest, and following Christ can be similar. The Christian life is a long journey that involves seeking God's kingdom by turning away from sin and turning to Christ again and again.

When John the Baptist came to announce God's kingdom, he said, "'The time has come . . . The kingdom of God has come near. Repent and believe the good news!'" (Mark 1:15). Repenting and believing are essential parts of following Jesus. But what does it mean to repent?

Repentance begins with seeing our sin clearly. It means being honest about what you've thought, said, or done, and not making excuses. Even though we feel sad and heartbroken, we must be honest and recognize that our sin has offended God and hurt other people.

Repentance also means actively turning away from sin. Repentance isn't just a change in attitude. It's also a change in behavior. We must turn away from our sin decisively, hating it, and wanting nothing to do with it.

Finally, repentance means turning to Jesus. When we repent, we turn our backs to living as rebels against God, and pledge our full allegiance to Jesus as our king. When we repent and believe the good news, our journey with Jesus begins. But that doesn't mean repentance stops. Because followers of Jesus still sin, we must repent again and again.

THINK ABOUT IT

• Reread the quote from Martin Luther on the previous page. Put it in your own words. Why is repentance so important for the Christian?

>>> PRAY: *Father, we find sin and temptation on our path every day. Through your Holy Spirit, help us turn from sin and turn to Jesus. Amen.*

What does it mean to have faith?

To trust only Jesus to save.

MEMORY VERSE:
Now faith is confidence in what we hope for and assurance about what we do not see.
Hebrews 11:1

Power-up Question:
When have you demonstrated trust in a friend while playing a game together? Tell about it.

>>> READ HEBREWS 11
AND ROMANS 4:16-24

> One believing sight of Christ is worth a thousand looks within ourselves. —Octavius Winslow

Abraham had amazing faith, but also had doubts. Just like you and me, Abraham sometimes struggled to trust God. Sometimes he followed his own ideas and his own understanding instead of trusting God's promises. When he grew tired of waiting for God's promises to come true, he disobeyed God (Genesis 16).

But when we read the books of Hebrews and Romans, it almost sounds like Abraham was perfect. Romans 4:20 says, "He did not waver through unbelief regarding the promise of God, but was strengthened in his faith and gave glory to God." How can this be? How can God look at someone who committed terrible sins and count them faithful?

Martin Luther once compared faith to an engagement ring. What makes the ring valuable isn't the size of the ring or what it's made of. It could be big or little; it might be made of gold, but it could also be made of wood or tin. No, what gives the ring value is the gem. If it's holding an expensive diamond, then it's an expensive ring!

The same is true of our faith. What matters most is not the size or strength of your faith. It's who you're putting your faith in. If your faith is holding onto Christ . . . if you are trusting only Jesus, then you have saving faith.

That's the point that Hebrews and Romans are making about Abraham. Abraham and Sarah were very old. Abraham's body was worn out and "as good as dead" (Romans 4:19; Hebrews 11:12). They couldn't have children. But they trusted that God was strong enough to give life to their aging bodies. So, Isaac was born when Sarah was 90 years old and Abraham was 100. Abraham wasn't strong, but he trusted the promises of our mighty God—who gives life to those who are as good as dead.

THINK ABOUT IT

• Think together about other Bible stories where God gave life to someone who was "as good as dead."

>>> PRAY: *Father, thank you for being the God who raises the dead. Thank you for raising your Son Jesus from the dead, and thank you for raising us into new life! Amen.*

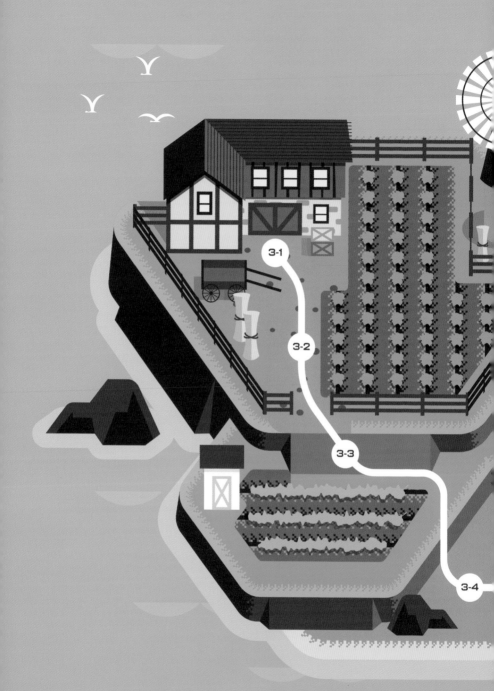

What is the gospel?

The good news that God graciously rescues us from sin and welcomes us into his kingdom because Jesus died and rose again.

MEMORY VERSE:
For God so loved the world that he gave his one and only Son, that whoever believes in him shall not perish but have eternal life. John 3:16

Power-up Question:
What's the most impressive structure you've ever created in a building game?

>>> **READ 1 CORINTHIANS 15:1-5**

 The gospel proclaims that the God who saved Israel from Egypt, Jonah from the fish's belly, the psalmist from death . . . saves all who trust Christ from sin and sin's consequences. —J. I. Packer

When you're building a structure, whether you're building a house with Legos, in Roblox, or Minecraft, it's essential to have a strong and level foundation. If the bottom layer isn't flat, or if the corners don't match up, every block you set on top will be wobbly. The same is true of our faith. We must be clear on the truths of the gospel. Otherwise, everything else will crumble. So, what is our gospel foundation?

First, the gospel is good news about God's kingdom! It's the good news that God has rescued his people from sin through his Son, Jesus. The Bible says that apart from Christ, we were "by nature children of wrath" (Ephesians 2:3 ESV). We deserved death and eternal punishment because of our sin. But God didn't leave us without a way of escape. He sent Jesus to rescue us from the dominion of darkness and welcome us into his glorious kingdom (Colossians 1:13).

Second, the gospel tells us how Jesus rescued us—through his death and resurrection. This is the good news: "that Christ died for our sins according to the Scriptures, that he was buried, that he was raised on the third day according to the Scriptures" (1 Corinthians 15:3a–4). When he died on the cross for us, Jesus took the punishment our sins deserved. When he rose from the grave, he gave us new life!

Finally, all this is possible only by God's grace. We didn't deserve any of this good news. It was a gracious rescue. In fact, there's nothing we can do on our own to earn forgiveness and freedom from sin. No matter how well we listen, how many chores we do, or how many nice things we say, none of that is enough to earn or deserve forgiveness. Only God has the power to forgive our sins and welcome us back into his kingdom.

THINK ABOUT IT

• Take turns sharing the gospel message in your own words.

>>> **PRAY:** *Father, thank you for the gift of the gospel. Thank you for reaching out to us when we were dead in sin and giving us life through your Son Jesus. Help us to build on a firm foundation of faith. Amen.*

What hope does the message of the gospel offer us?

Forgiveness of sins and life with Jesus forever.

MEMORY VERSE:
Therefore, there is now no condemnation for those who are in Christ Jesus, because through Christ Jesus the law of the Spirit who gives life has set you free from the law of sin and death. Romans 8:1–2

Power-up Question:
Who has been your friend the longest?

>>> READ ROMANS 8

> You see, no matter what, in spite of everything, God would love his children—with a Never Stopping, Never Giving Up, Unbreaking, Always and Forever Love. —Sally Lloyd-Jones

One fun thing about the Super Mario Brothers' mushroom kingdom is the search for extra lives. Extra lives come through collecting coins and finding the green 1UP mushrooms. You can also get an extra life by knocking off eight enemies in a row with a Koopa Troopa shell.

Jesus offers us something better than video game lives that don't run out. He offers us a qualitatively different kind of life—eternal life. Romans 8 teaches us that life with Jesus means:

Forgiveness. Paul says, "There is now no condemnation for those who are in Christ Jesus" (v. 1). Our sins deserve God's judgment, but Jesus lived perfectly and took our judgment upon himself. So, we no longer have to experience condemnation and punishment for our sins.

New citizenship. We were once citizens in the kingdom of self and sin. Romans 8 tells us, "Those who are in the realm of the flesh cannot please God" (v. 8). But the good news is that Christ has given us his Spirit so that we can live as citizens of his kingdom (v. 9). We're no longer trapped in slavery to our flesh; we can live new lives of obedience to God.

Adoption. Paul says, "Those who are led by the Spirit of God are the children of God" (v. 14). Because we have Jesus's Spirit, we call his Father, our Father. We belong to his household, the family of faith, and we'll enjoy the family inheritance with Jesus forever!

God is on our side. None of our present sufferings or sin, trauma or temptation can take away the wonderful new life Jesus offers to us. "In all things God works for the good of those who love him, who have been called according to his purpose" (v. 28).

That's better than a few 1UP mushrooms!

• What promise from Romans 8 is most meaningful to you?

>>> PRAY: *Father, thank you for your unstoppable love. Thank you for adopting us into your family. Thank you for making us citizens in your kingdom. Thank you for forgiving our sins so that we can have life with you forever. Amen.*

With what words do we confess our faith in the gospel?

In the words of the Apostles' Creed:
I believe in God, the Father almighty, creator of heaven and earth.

I believe in Jesus Christ, his only Son, our Lord. He was conceived by the Holy Spirit and born of the Virgin Mary. He suffered under Pontius Pilate, was crucified, died, and was buried. He descended to the dead. On the third day, he rose again. He ascended into heaven and is seated at the right hand of God the Father almighty. He will come again to judge the living and the dead.

I believe in the Holy Spirit, the holy Christian church, the communion of saints, the forgiveness of sins, the resurrection of the body, and the life everlasting. Amen.

MEMORY VERSE:
There is one body and one Spirit, just as you were called to one hope when you were called; one Lord, one faith, one baptism; one God and Father of all, who is over all and through all and in all. Ephesians 4:4–6

Power-up Question:
If you could travel back in time to live in any historical era, which era would you choose?

>>> RE-READ THE APOSTLES' CREED

> *[The Apostles' Creed] very ably summarizes the gospel in just a few sentences.* —D. A. Carson

The Apostles' Creed is a beautiful statement of our common faith. Each of the three parts of the creed begins with the words, *I believe,* because the creed summarizes our Christian beliefs. It puts the faith the apostles passed down to us into a few brief lines. Each of the three parts of the creed are related to one person of the Godhead. The longest part focuses on Jesus, because his birth, life, death, resurrection, and ascension for us is what accomplished our salvation.

If the Apostles' Creed is a summary of our Christian faith, how are we to use it today? The creed was initially designed as a tool to help the church teach the gospel to new believers. Many catechisms like *Luther's Small Catechism* and the *Heidelberg Catechism* include the creed, and many Christian traditions—like Anglicans, Lutherans, and Methodists—ask new converts to affirm the creed when they are baptized.

The creed reminds us that we're part of a long Christian history. Since the earliest days of the church, the creeds have been used in worship. They help us teach and pass on the good news that was taught to us. When we recite the creed during worship or before baptism, we're remembering, as Paul wrote, "There is one body and one Spirit, just as you were called to one hope when you were called; one Lord, one faith, one baptism; one God and Father of all, who is over all and through all and in all" (Ephesians 4:4–6).

THINK ABOUT IT

- This week, try to memorize the Apostles' Creed.
- Why do you think it's good to rehearse creeds and confessions in worship?

>>> **PRAY:** *Father, thank you for being the God of history. Thank you for the many Christians who have gone before us, and for the beautiful faith they've shared with us. Amen.*

What makes Jesus's life different from every other man?

Jesus was fully God and fully man, and he obeyed his Father perfectly.

MEMORY VERSE:
And Jesus grew in wisdom and stature, and in favor with God and man. Luke 2:52

Power-up Question:
Which video game character do you think is the most unique?

>>> READ LUKE 2:41-52

> Being human, Jesus could not conquer temptation without a struggle, but being divine it was his nature to do his Father's will. —J. I. Packer

In *Where in the World is Carmen Sandiego?* players travel around the world—or across time— looking for clues to find the dastardly villain. What if we were given a similar mission to travel back to Bible times to find Jesus? Would it be easy?

In Luke 2, Joseph, Mary, and their family traveled from their home in Nazareth to Jerusalem. On their return trip, Jesus went missing. So, Mary and Joseph began looking for him. After three days of searching high and low, they found Jesus in the temple in Jerusalem sitting among the teachers. Everyone there who heard him was amazed at his understanding and his answers. When Mary asked, "'Son, why have you treated us like this? Your father and I have been anxiously searching for you'" (v. 48), Jesus answered, "'Why were you searching for me? Didn't you know I had to be in my Father's house?'" (v. 49).

In his humanity, Jesus was like any ordinary child, but what makes Jesus different is that God is his Father.

Jesus is fully God. John 1:1 calls Jesus the Word, and it teaches us that Jesus is equal to his Father in power and in glory. Jesus is fully God. He always existed with the Father and the Holy Spirit before time began.

Jesus is fully man. The Son of God took on a human body and was born as a baby. He laughed, cried, ate, and slept. He was human in every way. Yet he remained fully God. His coming as a human—what we call the *incarnation*—didn't cause Jesus to lose his divine nature. In the incarnation, Jesus gained a human nature.

Jesus lived a sinless life. Because he was fully human, Jesus felt pain and faced temptation. But Jesus is different from every other human person who has lived because he never sinned. Jesus has always done the will of his Father.

THINK ABOUT IT

• Why is it important for Jesus to be both fully God and fully human?

>>> PRAY: *Jesus, you didn't regard equality with God as something to be used to your advantage, but in obedience to the Father, you became human to win our salvation. Thank you.*

How did Jesus die, and what happened after he died?

Jesus suffered the painful and
shameful death of the cross, but
after three days, he rose again!

MEMORY VERSE:
He then began to teach them that the Son of Man
must suffer many things . . . and that he must be
killed and after three days rise again. Mark 8:31

Power-up Question:
What's the worst level, death, or boss,
you've ever encountered in a video game?

>>> READ MARK 8:31-33

66 *If the cross is not central to our religion, ours is not the religion of
Jesus.* —*John Stott*

It was one of my (Trey's) first *Minecraft* playthroughs. I'd built an awesome hidden castle and found all the diamonds I needed for armor and tools. I'd enchanted everything, hit the Nether world, and began my search for a fortress. Then my wife Annie walked into the house from a grocery run. I set my controller down to help her get everything unloaded, but as I did, I bumped the joystick and my guy plummeted to his death. I lost all my levels and all my precious gear! When your character dies in a video game, it can seem frustrating, disappointing, and even devastating. That's how Jesus's disciples reacted when he predicted his death in Mark 8:31. Peter in particular couldn't believe it, and he tried to talk Jesus out of it. But Jesus was clear that his death and resurrection must take place. Why? Because his death had meaning.

Jesus's death is important because it's the only way our sins can be forgiven. The sin we inherited from Adam and Eve, as well as the sin we commit ourselves, deserves God's punishment. There's nothing we can do to escape this punishment. We need a Savior. God the Father, in his wisdom, sent his own Son, Jesus, to be our substitute and redeemer. Jesus took our sin upon himself by suffering a painful and shameful death on the cross. He took the punishment we deserved so we could be forgiven.

When Jesus spoke to his disciples, he also predicted his resurrection. Imagine the biggest, scariest, most difficult enemy you've ever faced in a game. Satan and sin are far worse! But Jesus beats them every time! Even death could not stand up to Jesus's power and might. The grave could only hold him for three days before he returned to life and appeared to his friends. In John 11, Jesus gives this promise to his followers: "I am the resurrection and the life. The one who believes in me will live, even though they die" (v. 25). This is our hope. Jesus is alive, and those who follow him enjoy both life with him today, and everlasting life in the resurrection.

THINK ABOUT IT

• How do we celebrate Jesus's resurrection today?

>>> **PRAY:** *Father, thank you for the gift of your Son, Jesus, and his death in our place. Thank you for the offer of grace that his life, death, and resurrection extend to us. Amen.*

Where is Jesus now?

He is in heaven where he rules with God the Father.

When will Jesus return?

He is coming soon, but we don't know when.
Come Lord Jesus.

MEMORY VERSE:
Since, then, you have been raised with Christ, set your hearts on things above, where Christ is, seated at the right hand of God. When Christ, who is your life appears, then you also will appear with him in glory.
Colossians 3:1, 4

Power-up Question:
Name the last video game, movie, or show you looked forward to coming out.

>>> READ ACTS 1:1-11

His exit from this life was as miraculous as his entrance.
—Paul E. Little

The game *Superman Returns* begins with an article by Daily Planet reporter, Lois Lane. She writes, "For five long years the world has stared into the sky—waiting, hoping, and praying for his return. We have spent our days asking where he went. Debating why he left and wondering if he is even alive . . . on the anniversary of his disappearance one question remains: Where is Superman?" As Christians, we should resonate with movies and games that focus on a character's big return, because our lives involve waiting, too.

After Jesus rose from the dead, he appeared to his disciples for forty days, teaching them about God's kingdom. The disciples thought it must finally be time for Jesus to restore political power to Israel. Jesus told his disciples to stay in Jerusalem and wait for the gift God promised them. Then, Jesus left them. The disciples stood and watched as Jesus rose up into the clouds until they couldn't see him anymore (Acts 1:9).

The disciples must've watched in amazement and sadness as the Savior left them. Where did Jesus go? Did he abandon them? In John 16, Jesus told his disciples that he would return to the Father. When Jesus *ascended*, he was *exalted* and *seated* at the Father's right hand with all power and authority (Luke 22:69; Acts 2:33).

Jesus didn't abandon his followers—like Superman seemingly abandoned the people of Metropolis. No, when Jesus ascended to heaven, he sent his Spirit. The Holy Spirit dwells within every follower of Christ. He helps believers understand God's Word, gives them spiritual gifts to serve the church, and empowers them to be witnesses of the gospel. Also, in heaven, Jesus prays for his people, ensuring they will be saved completely (Romans 8:34; Hebrews 7:23–25).

After Jesus ascended to heaven, two angels appeared and told the disciples that Jesus would return in the same way he had left (Acts 1:11). There will be a day when Jesus will come as conquering King. He will save his people and put an end to evil once for all. As we await Jesus's return, the Spirit empowers the church to advance God's kingdom by being witnesses of the gospel through our words and our actions.

THINK ABOUT IT

• How does Christ's promised return affect you? How does it give you hope?

⟫⟫ PRAY: *Jesus, you ascended into heaven. You sat down at the right hand of God the Father. You pray for us. You are coming soon. Come quickly, Lord Jesus. Come quickly.*

What did Jesus's life and work accomplish?

Everything necessary to win salvation for us.

MEMORY VERSE:

For Christ also suffered once for sins, the righteous for the unrighteous, to bring you to God. He was put to death in the body but made alive in the Spirit.
1 Peter 3:18

Power-up Question:
What is one of your greatest accomplishments?

>>> READ ROMANS 5:6-11

> *Expiation means God's removed my filthiness. The Old Testament type was the goat into the wilderness . . .*
> *Propitiation means since the Lamb has died, His work is finished—God's wrath is satisfied.*
> *—Shai Linne, "Atonement Q&A"*

In the video game world, iconic characters accomplish amazing feats again and again. Our favorite plumber, Mario, rescues Princess Peach from another castle. Red defeats Gary, his archrival and fellow Pokemon master, in their final showdown. And Samus from the Metroid games uses her bounty hunter skills to save the galaxy from space pirates time and time again. As awesome as these achievements sound, they take place in a fantasy world. But what Jesus accomplished for us isn't fantasy!

Jesus gave all, doing everything necessary to win salvation for his people. First Peter 3:18 teaches us four big truths about what Jesus accomplished:

Jesus is our sacrifice: "*For Christ also suffered once for sins.*" God required Israel to offer sacrifices day after day for their sins, but when Jesus died, he offered himself as the perfect sacrifice—a better sacrifice than bulls and goats (Hebrews 10:4). God poured his wrath on Jesus so that he took our full punishment (*propitiation*) and made us completely clean (*expiation*). Through his sacrifice, our sins have been paid for once and for all (Hebrews 10:10–12).

Jesus is our righteousness: "*the righteous for the unrighteous.*" When we put our faith in Jesus, we are *justified*. God declares us to be in the right, seeing us just as he sees his Son (2 Corinthians 5:21).

Jesus is our reconciliation: "*to bring us to God.*" Sin put us at war with God. As our mediator, Jesus brings us back to God, restoring our relationship (Colossians 1:20).

Jesus is our victory: "*He was put to death in the body, but made alive by the Spirit.*" Jesus is alive, so we have victory! We've been set free from the power of sin. Christ has defeated Satan, sin, and death (1 Corinthians 15:54–57).

THINK ABOUT IT

• List some of the things Jesus has accomplished for us.

>>> PRAY: *Jesus, you are our sacrifice, our righteousness, our reconciliation, and our victory. Thank you for defeating Satan, sin, and death. Amen.*

LEVEL 4

GOD'S GRACE

What is God's grace?

God's love freely given to us in Jesus.

MEMORY VERSE:
But God demonstrates his own love for us in this: While we were still sinners, Christ died for us. Romans 5:8

Power-up Question:
When has someone—besides Jesus—shown you grace and mercy? Tell about that time.

>>> READ LUKE 15:11-31

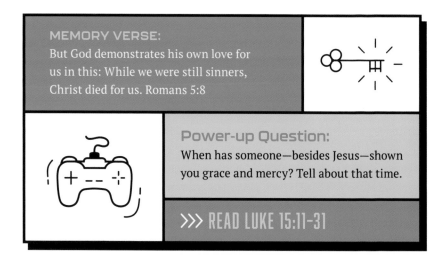

66 *What left a mark, no longer stings*
Because Grace makes beauty out of ugly things. —U2, "Grace"

I n Luke 15, Jesus paints a beautiful picture of God's grace in the parable of the prodigal son:

A father had two sons. One day the younger son asked his father to give him the share of his inheritance. A son usually received his inheritance after the father died, but this son wouldn't wait. He asked anyway. It was an act of great disrespect for his dad. And yet the father graciously gave his son his share.

After he got his money, the young son journeyed to a far country and wasted it all—every last penny! To make matters worse, the country where he went experienced a famine—a shortage of rain and food. With no money and no way to find food, the son was in trouble. Eventually, he had no choice but to take a job feeding pigs. Pigs disgusted him, but the son was so desperate and hungry that he hoped to eat some of the pigs' slop. Yuck!

Then the young man came to his senses and decided to return home and say, "Father, I've sinned against heaven and against you. I'm no longer worthy to be called your son. Make me like one of your hired workers."

When the son approached the father's house, the father saw him in the distance. He was filled with compassion and ran to embrace his son. The son started his apology, but his father cut him off. He said to his servants: "Quick! Bring the best robe and put it on him. Put a ring on his finger and sandals on his feet. Bring the fattened calf and kill it. Let's have a feast and celebrate. For this son of mine was dead and is alive again; he was lost and is found" (Luke 15:22–24).

Grace is the Father's wonderful acceptance of us, not because we have earned or deserve it, but because he freely gives it to us at Christ's expense. God didn't wait for us to clean ourselves up. He pursued us, dressed us in his righteousness, and threw a party. Even when we were his enemies, he showed his love by sending Jesus to die for us. That's amazing grace!

THINK ABOUT IT

- When the son in Luke 15 returns home, how does his father respond?
- Define the word "grace" in your own words.

>>> PRAY: *Father, thank you for loving us when we were still sinners. Thank you for sending Jesus to find us when we were lost. Amen.*

When did God choose to love and save his people?

God planned to love and save his people
before the creation of the world.

MEMORY VERSE:
For he chose us in him before the creation of the
world to be holy and blameless in his sight. In love
he predestined us for adoption to sonship through
Jesus Christ, in accordance with his pleasure and will.
Ephesians 1:4–5

Power-up Question:
What game was so challenging you needed
someone's help to complete it?

>>> READ ACTS 27:13-44

> *And you know the plans that you have for me*
> *And you can't plan the ends and not plan the means.*
> —Caedmon's Call, "Table for Two"

When I (Trey) was a kid, I enjoyed role playing video games like *Zelda* or *Final Fantasy*, but occasionally I'd get stuck. My character wasn't strong enough. I didn't have the proper equipment to survive the dungeon. What could I do? In those days, we didn't have YouTube, so I'd purchase video game magazines at the bookstore. The magazines included maps of each game's world along with charts that described all the armor, weapons, and skills I needed to make it through. They gave me a plan to get where I needed to go.

In Acts 27, Paul is imprisoned for his faith in Jesus. He's on a boat, headed to Rome to stand before Caesar. On the way, the Lord sends an angel to deliver a message to Paul. The angel reveals God's plan for the voyage—that there will be a shipwreck, but everyone aboard will survive. Paul doesn't receive every detail, but he hears God's word from the angel. He trusts that God will see him through.

We also can trust God's plans. Before he made the heavens and earth, God had a plan to save his people through the life, death, and resurrection of his Son, Jesus. This wasn't a last-minute plan God adopted after sin entered the picture. No, God knew exactly what he was doing from the start. He chose those he would save long before they took their first breaths. Not only that, but God chose exactly how he would save them. This is what we mean when we say that God *predestined* his people for salvation.

God's plan is always clear to him, but it's not always clear to us. Like the soldiers on Paul's ship, we're often tempted to panic when we face life's hardships and suffering. But we can trust God's good plans are working out whatever comes. He always sees his people safely through to the end.

THINK ABOUT IT

- How could Paul have confidence in the face of a shipwreck?
- What gives you confidence amid difficulty?

>>> **PRAY:** *God, thank you for choosing us before you created the world. Help us to trust your good plan for our lives and our salvation. Amen.*

Can you come to God in your own power?

No. We are dead in sin, and we need the Holy Spirit to make us alive.

MEMORY VERSE:
But because of his great love for us, God, who is rich in mercy, made us alive with Christ even when we were dead in transgressions—it is by grace you have been saved. Ephesians 2:4–5

Power-up Question:
What's the spookiest enemy you've had to overcome (or run away from!) in a game?

>>> READ EZEKIEL 37:1-14

> All people are now conceived in sin and born children of wrath, unfit for any saving good, inclined toward evil, dead in their sins, and slaves to sin; without the grace of the regenerating Holy Spirit, they are neither willing nor able to return to God. —Canons of Dort (3/4:3)

The Dry Bones enemies in *Super Mario Bros.* pace back and forth to prevent you from finding the boss in each castle. The skeletons in *Minecraft* will chase you down and shoot arrows at you. But in real life, dry bones aren't going anywhere by themselves. They have no muscles, no brain, and no heart. A skeleton may hang together on a stand in anatomy class, but the bones have no power to move on their own. Unless it's late in October, you're not going to see a skeleton walking around your neighborhood.

That's what makes the story in Ezekiel 37 so remarkable. God took the prophet to a valley filled with dry bones and asked, "Can these bones live?" (v. 3). Ezekiel was unsure: "Sovereign Lord, you alone know." Then, God commanded the prophet to preach to the bones: "Dry bones, hear the word of the Lord!" (v. 4). As Ezekiel preached, the bones came together, and God clothed the skeletons in flesh. The Lord breathed life into the dead bodies, and through the power of his Word, he made the dead skeletons alive! They turned into a great army!

The Bible teaches us that apart from God, we are dead in our sin (Ephesians 2:1–3). Left on our own, no person seeks God (Psalm 14:2–3; 53:2–3; Romans 3:11–12). The Bible isn't saying that people have no choice to make; it's reminding us that we want what we want. Apart from God's Spirit, we all follow our sinful wants and desires. "Each of us has turned to our own way" (Isaiah 53:6). "Our bones are dried up and our hope is gone" (Ezekiel 37:11b).

But then God's Word comes. We hear the good news through a friend or a preacher, and the Spirit says, "Live!" Suddenly, our stone-cold hearts begin to thaw and gradually they beat in rhythm with God's will. First, we see the peril and poison of our sin. Then, the eyes of our hearts blink open and we wake up to the beauty of Christ and his ways. It's a resurrection for our souls called *regeneration*. Praise God! We are made alive by his amazing grace.

THINK ABOUT IT

- What happened when Ezekiel preached to the bones?
- Can a dead skeleton move on its own? Why not?
- Apart from God's help, can we hear his voice?

>>> **PRAY:** *Holy Spirit, we are dead without you. Come and make us alive today so we live like you've raised us to live. Amen.*

Can you earn or deserve God's grace?

No! God gives us salvation as a free gift.

MEMORY VERSE:
For it is by grace you have been saved, through faith—and this is not from yourselves, it is the gift of God—not by works so that no one can boast. Ephesians 2:8–9

Power-up Question:
What is one of the best gifts you've ever received?

>>> READ EPHESIANS 2:1-10

---

66 *You contribute nothing to your salvation except for the sin that made it necessary.* —Jonathan Edwards

Did you know that some video games celebrate your birthday? In *Animal Crossing: New Horizons*, players receive free game rewards, a digital birthday cake, cupcakes, and a surprise party with a song! All to celebrate your special day.

God loves to shower his people with gifts, and his best gift is the gift of salvation. Ephesians 2:8–9 says, "For it is by grace you have been saved, through faith—and this is not from yourselves, it is the gift of God—not by works so that no one can boast."

This passage makes clear that God's gift of salvation is free. There is no amount of good work we can do to earn it. And we should never think that we're good enough to deserve it. We have no reason to brag or pat ourselves on the back, as if we received his gift through our own efforts, or because we were born into the right family.

God doesn't owe us anything, but he showed his love by sending Jesus to pay the full price for our sins. He promises redemption and forgiveness for those who will put their faith in him. But God doesn't only offer us the free gift of salvation by faith. Ephesians 2 says that God even gives us faith itself. "It is the gift of God."

God freely gives us faith and all its treasures. This is good news. If we had received what we deserved and earned, it would only be God's judgment and punishment for our sin. But instead of the wrath we deserved, God chose to send Jesus to save us. Before we did anything good or bad, God chose to redeem us in Christ.

Isn't it wonderful to receive Jesus as a perfectly free gift?

THINK ABOUT IT

• Name some of the great gifts you've received because of Jesus's death and resurrection. Take some time to give him thanks.

>>> **PRAY:** *God, thank you for the free gift of salvation in Jesus. Give us faith so we might continue to trust him. Amen.*

Who will come to God?

God's people know his voice, and they follow him.
We can't reach God, but he reaches us.

MEMORY VERSE:
"My sheep listen to my voice; I know them, and they follow me." John 10:27

Power-up Question:
What's your favorite form of video-game travel (car, horse, airship, zipline, etc.)?

>>> READ ACTS 9:1-22

Rebirth quickens someone to spiritual life in such a way that Jesus is now seen in his irresistible sweetness. —R. C. Sproul

In *Zelda: Breath of the Wild*, our hero, Link, begins the game by exploring a giant plateau. When he walks to its edges, he can see a larger world beneath him. There's one problem. The drop to the world below seems impossible to span. How can Link cross it? Suddenly, a wise old man appears to guide Link. He offers Link just what he needs—a glider that will help him take the plunge to the new world below, and his voice to guide the way.

Saul was wandering like Link on that plateau, but he didn't know he was stuck. After all, Saul had chased God his entire life (Philippians 3:4–6), trying to please God by being a good Pharisee. Saul was certain Jesus's disciples were wrong about God. He went out of his way to chase them down and imprison them. Then, Jesus appeared to Saul and changed everything he thought he knew. The bright light blinded Saul's physical eyes, but meeting Jesus opened the eyes of his heart (Acts 9:17–22). Saul began to see his sin. He discovered that his lifelong pursuit had taken him further away from God instead of closer. He met the Lord, and the world opened up to him in a new way. Jesus sent Saul out on a new quest as his chosen instrument to proclaim his name before both Jews and Gentiles (v. 15).

Apart from a personal encounter with Jesus, we're like Saul on the way to Damascus. We might have heard about Jesus, read our Bibles, and heard sermons preached, but we have not met him. Thankfully, God doesn't leave us to wander alone. Like Link on the edge of that plateau, we can't reach God on our own, but when he calls, we answer and follow. The more we hear about the goodness and greatness of salvation in Jesus, the more irresistible he becomes. Though we are sinners who run away from God, he goes out of his way to find us. He opens our eyes. We hear his voice more clearly, and the Spirit changes our rebellion into complete surrender.

THINK ABOUT IT

• When are you most tempted to rebel against your parents?

• Where have you experienced God's grace?

>>> PRAY: *Father, show me my sin, and help me to trust in you. Transform my rebellion into obedience. Amen.*

How do I know I belong to God?

The Holy Spirit bears witness that we are God's children forever.

MEMORY VERSE:
When you believed, you were marked in him with a seal, the promised Holy Spirit, who is a deposit guaranteeing our inheritance until the redemption of those who are God's possession—to the praise of his glory. Ephesians 1:13b–14

Power-up Question:
When you feel unsafe, where do you go? Do you have a favorite place where you find comfort (in your room, home, yard, etc.)?

>>> READ JOHN 10:27-30

*Earthly cares forever vex me, while thy trials lay me low;
But when Satan comes to tempt me, to that secret place I go.*
—Sandra McCracken, "In the Secret of His Presence"

How do you feel when you find a safe place in a video game? By *safe place*, I mean the parts in the game's world—your base in *Minecraft*, villages in the *Zelda* games, or any of the many safe places in the Lego games—where you can catch your breath because you're protected from danger.

If you appreciate that feeling, I have good news for you. When you put your trust in Jesus Christ, the Holy Spirit marks you safe with Jesus! Paul explained to the Ephesians, "When you believed, you were marked in [Christ] with a seal, the promised Holy Spirit" (Ephesians 1:13b). The Holy Spirit marks us as part of God's family, guaranteeing that all his promises will come true (v. 14). Jesus promises us that no one will snatch us out of the Father's hand (John 10:27–30). The Holy Spirit protects us so we'll never be lost. He keeps us safe and secure with Jesus forever.

The Holy Spirit is far safer than the safest place in any video game. In games, when you leave the place of safety, you're at the mercy of the enemies who might come after you. But the Holy Spirit is with us when we face Satan's temptations and our own sinful desires. The Bible even promises us that the Holy Spirit will be with us when we face death.

Whenever we're tempted to believe Satan's lies, the Spirit brings God's truth to our minds. He reminds us of the truth we've been taught from the Bible (John 14:26). When we sin, the Spirit exposes our guilt and failure (John 16:8). But this doesn't mean God has left us. In love, God reveals our sin. When he corrects us, it's because he loves us and longs to make us more like himself.

When we feel anxious and doubt God's love, the Spirit comforts us. He reminds us that we belong to God as his sons and daughters. As Paul writes in Romans, "The Spirit testifies with our spirit that we are God's children" (8:16). We hear and listen to the Spirit, like sheep following their good shepherd. In so many ways, the Holy Spirit keeps us. He's our comfort and assurance. He ministers Christ's presence and truth. We must find our safety with him.

THINK ABOUT IT

- How do you know God loves you?
- What evidence of God's love do you see in your own life?

>>> **PRAY:** *Father, your love never fails. Thank you for sending the Holy Spirit as the seal of your love. Thank you for keeping us safe in Jesus. Amen.*

What is growth in Christ?

Growth is a lifelong partnership with the Holy Spirit to change and become like Jesus.

Does God only change us a little?

No. The Holy Spirit changes our whole life.

MEMORY VERSE:
Do not be conformed to this world, but be transformed by the renewal of your mind, that by testing you may discern what is the will of God, what is good and acceptable and perfect. Romans 12:2 ESV

Power-up Question:
What is your favorite power up in a video game?

>>> READ ROMANS 12:1-21

His strength is perfect when our strength is gone.
He'll carry us when we can't carry on.
Raised in his power, the weak become strong.
His strength is perfect. —Stephen Curtis Chapman

ince the days of *Pac-Man*, gamers have been on a quest for power. Whether it's the star man in *Super Mario Bros.*, a bottled fairy in Hyrule, or catching "On fire!" in *NBA Jam*, gamers are looking for special items and opportunities that transform their abilities and give them strength to conquer enemies. The change a power up brings can make all the difference!

We also need power to grow and live as Christians—power to defeat sin, power to love others, and power to follow God's will. For this reason, God has given his people the Holy Spirit. The Spirit doesn't only change us a little. No. God's Holy Spirit changes a Christian's entire life!

Change in the Christian life often begins with the way we think. Apart from the Holy Spirit's work, our minds conform to the patterns of this world. But the Holy Spirit uses God's Word to transform our minds and change our outlook so that we're no longer focused on ourselves but have the mind of Christ (1 Corinthians 2:6–16).

As we behold Christ's beauty and glory in the Bible, we become like him. The Spirit gives us new attitudes and affections. Because we love Christ, we learn to hate what is evil and cling to what is good. Our actions and behavior change as well. We honor God's people, practice hospitality, and care for their needs. We have lives that are characterized by love, joy, patience, gentleness, and peacemaking. We are not overcome by evil, but we overcome evil with good (Galatians 5:22–23; Romans 12:9–21).

The Spirit's power is different from a video game power up. God's power is never a weapon that gives us *power over* other people made in God's image. Rather, it's the power to serve and love others even when we feel weak.

Also, God's power isn't always easy to see. Being filled with the Spirit won't make you flash different colors like Mario does when he finds a star. No one may notice the times when God's power is most at work in you. But that's okay. In quiet obedience and unnoticed acts of love, God is powerfully at work to make you more like him.

THINK ABOUT IT

- When do you feel strong? When do you feel weak?
- When is God's strength most evident?

>>> PRAY: *Father, your strength is perfect. Show your great power in our weakness, and help us grow up into maturity in Christ. Amen.*

What means does the Holy Spirit use to change Christians?

Prayer, God's Word, and trials.

MEMORY VERSE:

Teach me, Lord, the way of your decrees, that I may follow it to the end. Give me understanding, so that I may keep your law and obey it with all my heart. Psalm 119:33–34

Your word is a lamp for my feet, a light on my path. Psalm 119:105

Power-up Question:
What would you like to learn how to build?

>>> READ PSALM 119:25-40

For as soon as God's Word takes root and grows in you, the devil will harry you, and will make a real doctor of you, and by his assaults will teach you to seek and love God's Word. —Martin Luther

In *Minecraft*, you've got access to a handful of tools—an axe, sword, hoe, and shovel. You can use them to build almost any structure imaginable. Beginners start with tiny box-shaped houses but can eventually craft an enormous castle or sweeping resort. Whatever you build, it all begins with those simple tools.

Throughout our lives as Christians, the Holy Spirit is at work making us more like Christ. The Spirit uses three key tools to grow and shape us into a masterpiece: prayer, God's Word, and trials. We see all three in Psalm 119.

Through *prayer*, we communicate our fears, joys, hopes, and disappointments to God. We also ask the Lord to hear us and make us into disciples who love his Word and want to obey his will. In Psalm 119, David prays, "Teach me your decrees" (v. 26b). Again and again, he says, "Instruct me. Lead me. Show me." We can be confident that when we pray these prayers, God will answer us (1 John 5:14). The Holy Spirit opens our eyes to understand God's Word and will.

In *his Word*, God teaches us about himself, the world he created, and how we are to live in it. David tells us that God's Word is a lamp for our feet and a light for our path (v. 105). As we read, study, and memorize passages from the Bible, God uses his Word to change us. Whether we're young or old, a pastor or a student, a new believer or an old saint, we never outgrow our need to read, hear, sing, and speak the Scriptures.

Finally, we grow through *trials and suffering*. At some point in life, we all face difficult and unexpected circumstances—a friend treats you badly, a pet dies without warning, or you have to move and go to a new school. But as we live out God's Word in difficult circumstances, we are changed. As we trust God through suffering, we're changed into his image day after day.

THINK ABOUT IT

• How has the Holy Spirit used suffering to change you?

>>> PRAY: *Father, thank you for sending your Spirit to instruct, empower, and change us. Thank you for providing ways we can hear your voice and respond. Amen.*

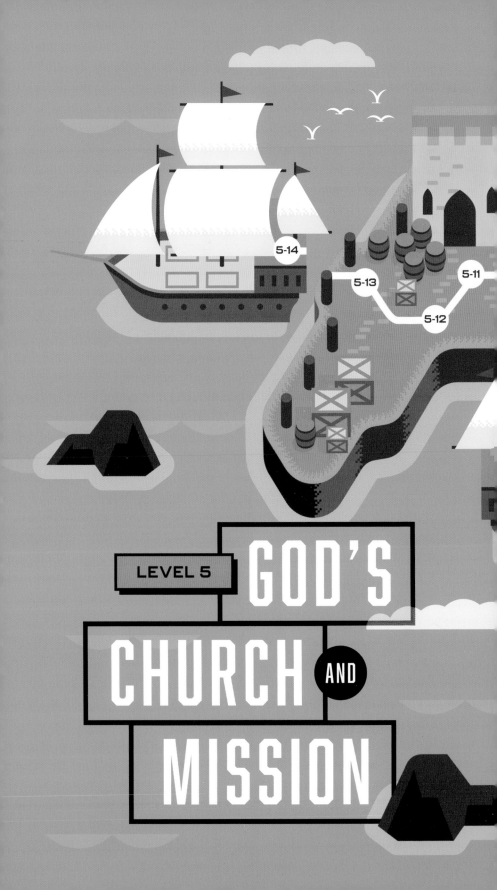

LEVEL 5 GOD'S CHURCH AND MISSION

5-14

5-13

5-12

5-11

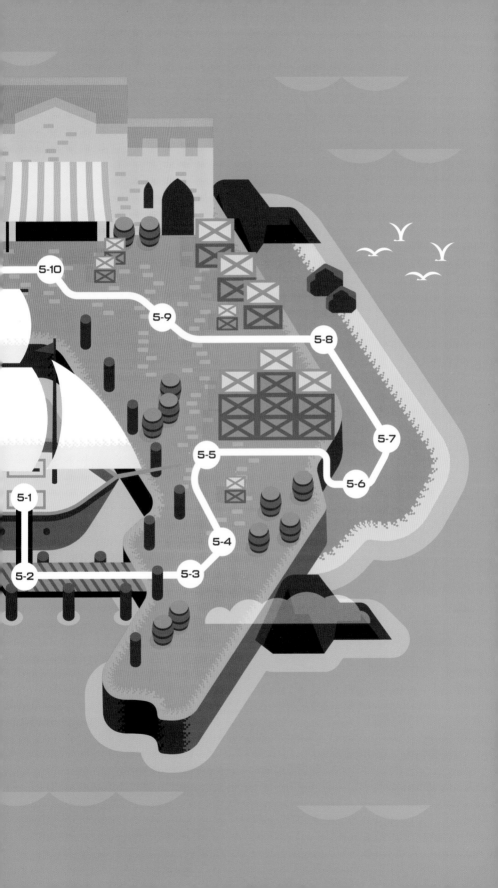

What is the church?

The church is the people that
God has made alive, called together,
and sent on mission together.

MEMORY VERSE:
But you are a chosen people, a royal priesthood, a
holy nation, God's special possession, that you may
declare the praises of him who called you out of
darkness into his wonderful light. 1 Peter 2:9

Power-up Question:
What video games require teamwork?

>>> READ 1 PETER 2:4-10

*God has prepared for Himself one great song of praise throughout
eternity, and those who enter the community of God join in this song.*
—Dietrich Bonhoeffer

When the fate of the Marvel world is at stake, earth's mightiest heroes, the Avengers, assemble to face the threat. This team of superheroes brings their powers and abilities from across the universe. On their own, each Avenger is a force to be reckoned with. Together, they're unstoppable.

In God's Word, we discover a group of people—an assembly—who God has made alive, called together, and sent out with a common mission. This group of heroes is the church. Sometimes when we hear the word *church*, we think of a building with big front doors and a steeple or two. But when the Bible talks about the church, it is talking about the people of God, those who trust Christ in the past, present, and future.

Made alive. Peter tells us the church is a holy and chosen people (1 Peter 2:9). We once lived in darkness, dead in our sins. But God brought us into the light by making us alive in Christ. Now we belong to God as his treasured people (v. 10).

Called together. When we follow Jesus, we not only belong to God, we also belong to his people. The church is where people from different backgrounds and walks of life become one family. Acts 2:42–47 describes how the early church lived in unity. The people came together regularly to pray and hear teaching from God's Word. They shared meals and even property. They cared for one another, enjoyed each other's company, and worshiped God together. This is the church united in one Spirit with one Lord, one faith, and one baptism (Ephesians 4:3–6).

Sent out on mission. Peter says the church is set apart "that you may declare the praises of him who called you out of darkness into his wonderful light" (1 Peter 2:9b). We are Christ's representatives who share his good news with the world!

THINK ABOUT IT

• Why do you think it's important for the church to be united?

>>> **PRAY:** *Father, thank you for calling us as your people. Jesus, may your peace be in our hearts so we can love each other as one united church. Spirit, fill us with your power to sing your praises to all people. Amen.*

Why is the church called family?

Because God is our Father, and Christ is our brother. We are God's adopted children, and we care for one another like brothers and sisters.

MEMORY VERSE:
To all who received him, who believed in his name, he gave power to become children of God. John 1:12

Power-up Question:
Who's your favorite fictional family? What makes them unique?

>>> READ ACTS 10

" Church membership is not simply a record of a box we once checked. It should be a record of a living commitment or it's worthless.
—Mark Dever

Peter was part of the *Jewish* family and nation. The Jewish people could only eat meat if it came from an animal with cloven hooves like a cow, sheep, goat, or deer. They weren't allowed to eat other animals (like pigs!). No bacon, hot dogs, or barbecue! Jewish people also wouldn't sit at the same table with Gentiles (people who weren't Jewish). These laws and customs kept God's people separate from foreign peoples who worshiped false gods.

Cornelius was a soldier in the *Roman* army. As a Gentile, he was free to eat whatever and with whomever he wanted, but Jewish people wouldn't eat with him. No, the Romans had invaded and taken over their land. No faithful Jew would visit a Roman soldier's house for a meal.

Peter and Cornelius were from completely different cultures. But they both loved God, so God put them together in one family. It all began with a dream. While Peter slept, God showed him a blanket filled with animals (like pigs!) they were not allowed to eat. God told Peter to eat the animals. God said, "Do not call anything impure that God has made clean" (Acts 10:15). When Peter woke up, there were visitors at his door. They invited Peter to Cornelius's home, and Peter went with them to tell Cornelius and his family about Jesus. Cornelius believed, and the two men even ate together!

Though the two men were from different nations and cultures, God adopted them both into his family. God is the Father of all who trust in Jesus. We might speak different languages, wear different clothes, have different hobbies, and eat different foods. But if we belong to God, we are part of his church! God is our Father, and Christ is our brother. We are God's adopted children, and we care for one another like siblings. We are part of one family!

THINK ABOUT IT

- Who is a part of God's family?
- How is God's family similar to your family?
- How is it different?

>>> **PRAY:** *God, thank you for welcoming all who trust Jesus into your forever family. Thank you for making a way for us to know you, our heavenly Father. Amen.*

Why are Christians called servants?

Because Jesus is our Lord. We serve others because Christ first served us.

MEMORY VERSE:
Therefore, I urge you, brothers and sisters, in view of God's mercy, to offer your bodies as a living sacrifice, holy and pleasing to God—this is your true and proper worship. Romans 12:1

Power-up Question:
What qualities make a video game character great?

>>> READ ACTS 6:1-8:1

> Wherever he leads, I'll go. Wherever he leads, I'll go.
> I'll follow my Christ who loves me so. Wherever he leads, I'll go.
> —B. B. Mckinney

In the book of Acts, we read about the growth of the early church. Many people heard the gospel, and many more believed. Soon there were too many people for the apostles to care for on their own. So, the leaders chose seven men to help. After these men were chosen, even more people believed in Jesus, and the church kept growing.

One of the seven chosen servants was named Stephen. He was full of the Holy Spirit, wisdom, and faith. God empowered Stephen as a teacher and used him to perform miracles. Stephen taught the people how Jesus died and rose for our salvation.

Stephen's teaching made some of the Jews angry. They made up lies about him, saying, "'We have heard Stephen speak blasphemous words against Moses and against God'" (Acts 6:11). Stephen answered these lies by telling the people the truth: He said that the Jewish leaders had disobeyed God, rejected God's prophets, and also killed Jesus, the Messiah.

This made the Jewish leaders even more angry! They picked up stones to throw at Stephen; they wanted to kill him. How did Stephen respond? He served them by praying for them. As Stephen died, he prayed, "Lord, do not hold this sin against them" (Acts 7:60).

Jesus didn't come to be served, but to serve and help others. Christians follow Christ's example by loving and serving others. Like Stephen, sometimes Christians serve others by giving their lives.

Serving is *not* only doing chores like washing the dishes or cleaning our rooms. No, serving is part of our identity as Christians. We do *not* serve to make people happy. No, when we serve others, we are serving the Lord. We do *not* serve to earn God's approval. No, God has given us his love in Jesus Christ. Because of this, we can serve sacrificially and with a grateful heart.

THINK ABOUT IT

• Do you find joy in serving others, or is it more like a chore? Why do you think that's the case?

>>> **PRAY:** *Jesus, you are the Servant of All. Help us serve as you first served us. Amen.*

How is the church empowered as a witness?

The Holy Spirit fills Christians and helps us share Jesus with others.

MEMORY VERSE:

"Therefore go and make disciples of all nations, baptizing them in the name of the Father and of the Son and of the Holy Spirit." Matthew 28:19

"But you will receive power when the Holy Spirit comes on you; and you will be my witnesses in Jerusalem, and in all Judea and Samaria, and to the ends of the earth." Acts 1:8

Power-up Question:
What was your favorite mission in a video game?

>>> READ MATTHEW 28:16-20

> *Mission is God's own going forth . . . He is Sender, Sent, and Sending.*
> —R. Paul Stephens

In the *Marvel's Spider-Man: Miles Morales* game, Peter Parker trains young Miles to be the new Spider-Man. At the beginning of the game, Peter tells Miles that he'll need to leave New York for a while. Miles is afraid because he doesn't feel like he's ready to be Spider-Man. Peter encourages him, because he knows Miles is equipped and ready for the mission.

Our mission as followers of Jesus is to be his witnesses. To fulfill this command, we must go into all they world, proclaim the gospel, and make disciples. This command is called the Great Commission. But we've misunderstood it if we think it's only something we're commanded to do. God's mission didn't begin in Matthew 28. God himself was on mission long before he welcomed his people to join.

The Father sent the Son (John 3:16–17; 5:36); the Father and Son send the Holy Spirit (14:26; 15:26); and now we are sent into the world (20:21; cf. Acts 1:8). God's mission is from the Father, through the Son, and by the Holy Spirit. Being witnesses means joining God in a mission he's already at work to complete.

Jesus reminded his disciples about this truth when he told them, "And surely I am with you always, to the very end of the age'" (Matthew 28:20). Our witness is empowered by the Holy Spirit. He equips us and makes us ready. Yes, the church is commanded to go and make disciples by teaching and baptizing, but the Spirit goes with us! We are never left alone.

THINK ABOUT IT

- Who in your life tells you about Jesus?
- When have you sensed Jesus's presence with you?

>>> **PRAY:** *God, thank you for choosing us to be witnesses of your amazing grace. Help us share the good news of Jesus with our friends and family this week. We want others to know how much you love them, and we want you to use us to tell them. Amen.*

What is baptism?

Going under the water in the name of the Father, the Son, and the Holy Spirit.

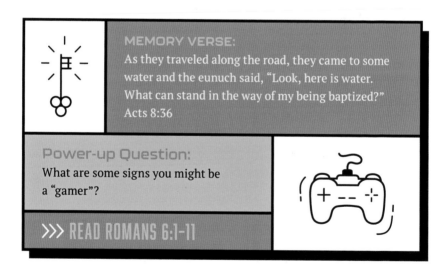

MEMORY VERSE:
As they traveled along the road, they came to some water and the eunuch said, "Look, here is water. What can stand in the way of my being baptized?"
Acts 8:36

Power-up Question:
What are some signs you might be a "gamer"?

>>> READ ROMANS 6:1-11

> *This water symbolizes baptism that now saves you also—not the removal of dirt from the body but the pledge of a clear conscience toward God. —1 Peter 3:21*

efore Jesus ascended to heaven, he gave his church two sacred rituals to celebrate until his return. The first is baptism. Baptism is going under water in the name of the Father, the Son, and the Holy Spirit. The rite of baptism teaches us the following:

Christians are united to Christ in his life, death, and resurrection. Romans 6 says we are united to Christ in faith and "baptized into his death" (v. 3). In some Christian traditions, new believers are immersed and then raised out of the water. This symbolizes a person's old, sinful life dying with Christ. Coming out of the water is a picture of being raised with Christ to a life of new obedience.

Christians are cleansed from sin. When Ananias preached to Paul, he commanded him, "Get up, be baptized and wash your sins away" (Acts 22:16). In some Christian traditions, water is sprinkled or poured over the head of infant children. Being washed with water teaches us about the cleansing power of God's grace.

Christians are saved from judgment. In the Old Testament, those who passed "through the waters" were saved from judgment (Isaiah 43:2). God rescued Noah through the flood. He rescued the people of Israel through the Red Sea. The New Testament authors see these events as early pictures of baptism (1 Corinthians 10:2; 1 Peter 3:21).

Christians are part of Christ's body, the church. Paul wrote, "For we were all baptized by one Spirit so as to form one body" (1 Corinthians 12:13a). Through baptism, we are united with God's people. We together share in a common faith as members of Christ's body (Ephesians 4:4).

Jesus said, "Go and make disciples of all nations, baptizing them in the name of the Father and of the Son and of the Holy Spirit" (Matthew 28:19). The church has obeyed for 2,000 years.

THINK ABOUT IT

• What is your favorite truth about baptism? Why?

>>> PRAY: *Father, help us to remember our baptism. Give us assurance that we've been united to Christ, cleansed from sin, saved from judgment, and welcomed into the church. Amen.*

What is Communion?

Eating bread and drinking the cup to remember Jesus's death until he comes.

MEMORY VERSE:
And he took bread, gave thanks and broke it, and gave it to them, saying, "This is my body given for you; do this in remembrance of me." In the same way, after the supper he took the cup, saying, "This cup is the new covenant in my blood, which is poured out for you." Luke 22:19–20

Power-up Question:
What would you make if were preparing a large feast in a cooking simulator game?

>>> READ LUKE 22:7-23

 Do this is remembrance of me. —1 Corinthians 11:24

In games like *Overcooked!* and *Diner Dash*, players rush to make meals for customers. The goal of these games is not to make quality food. It's to serve as many people as possible, as fast as you can. When we sit down for a holiday meal at Thanksgiving, the goal is different. We have traditional foods—like turkey, mashed potatoes and gravy, casseroles, and pies—that are carefully prepared. We're not in a rush. Instead, we take our time to enjoy making the food, eating it, and being with our family and friends.

Luke 22 shares how Jesus and his disciples celebrated a slow, traditional meal that God gave to his people during the time of Moses. They ate bread, herbs, lamb, and wine to remember how God had rescued the children of Israel from slavery (Exodus 12:1–30). This meal was called the Passover.

As Jesus and his disciples ate the Passover meal, Jesus also gave his disciples a new meal. He wanted them to remember how he came to save them from sin. So Jesus took the bread and said, "This is my body given for you." Then he took the cup and said, "This cup is the new covenant in my blood, which is poured out for you" (Luke 22:19–20). The new meal is called the Lord's Supper, or Communion.

Jesus knew the time had come for his betrayal, suffering, and death. The bread and wine were pictures of what was about to take place. The bread pictured Jesus's body, which would be broken. The cup pictured Jesus's blood, which would be shed for our forgiveness. It was a sign of the new relationship we have with God as his family. When we take Communion, we're remembering Jesus's death and the common faith we share with every believer who is a part of his family. Together, we're proclaiming the good news of how we've been saved from death and delivered from the bondage of sin. The church keeps this meal together until the day when Jesus returns.

THINK ABOUT IT

- How does Communion remind us of Jesus's death?
- How does it remind us of our unity with the church?

>>> **PRAY:** *Jesus, thank you for giving your life for the forgiveness of our sins. Thank you for making a way for us to have a new relationship with you.*

How does the church show its complete dependence on God?

Through prayer.
This is how Jesus taught us to pray.

MEMORY VERSE:
"Our Father in heaven, Hallowed be Your name. Your kingdom come. Your will be done, On earth as it is in heaven. Give us this day our daily bread. And forgive us our debts, As we forgive our debtors. And do not lead us into temptation, But deliver us from the evil one. For Yours is the kingdom and the power and the glory forever. Amen." Matthew 6:9–13 NKJV

Power-up Question:
Share a time you had difficulty completing a game level or mission. How did you overcome it?

>>> READ MATTHEW 6:5-15

> *We must bring our needs before God humbly, willing to submit to his perfect plan.* —R. Albert Mohler, Jr.

Do you like competing to get a high score in a video or arcade game? When you play video games, pinball, Skee-Ball, or Pop-A-Shot basketball at an arcade, you're competing with other players. If you score at the top, you might get your initials on the game's leader board. It can be fun to compete for a high score. When you've done a great job, it's natural to want to celebrate and share your success with others.

But what if you had that same attitude in talking to God? What if you bragged about being the best at prayer? Would that be a good idea? In Matthew 6:5–6, Jesus warned his disciples:

> "And when you pray, you must not be like the hypocrites. For they love to stand and pray in the synagogues and at the street corners, that they may be seen by others. Truly, I say to you, they have received their reward. But when you pray, go into your room and shut the door and pray to your Father who is in secret. And your Father who sees in secret will reward you."

Jesus wants us to know that prayer is not like *Pac-Man* or pinball. The point is not to be seen or tell others how great we are. Prayer is not a way to show off. No, it's just the opposite. Prayer is an opportunity to show just how needy we are. In prayer, we tell God that we are dependent upon him.

We can't save ourselves. We can't provide for ourselves without God's help. Before God, we're like newborn babies who can't feed, dress, or care for themselves. We need God, our good and loving Father, to hear us when we ask for healing, grace, forgiveness, provision, and help.

THINK ABOUT IT

• How often do you think about your need for God?

>>> **PRAY:** *Father, help us to see our great need for you. Help us to remember that you are a good and loving Father who loves to give good gifts to your children. Amen.*

What are we asking when we pray, "Hallowed be your name"?

That we might love God and praise his name above all things.

MEMORY VERSE:
I will give thanks to you, LORD, with all my heart;
I will tell of all your wonderful deeds. I will be glad
and rejoice in you; I will sing the praises of your name,
O Most High. Psalm 9:1–2

Power-up Question:
What would you say is the greatest
game ever? Why?

>>> READ MATTHEW 6:9, 19-24

The Lord's Prayer begins with the request, "*Hallowed* be your name." Hallowed is a tricky word that we don't often use. What does it mean? To hallow means to set apart as holy, sacred, and revered. When we pray these words, we're recognizing that God is beautiful and worthy of our praise. We're saying that God is above and more important than anything else we hold dear. Nothing we own, no relationship we have, nor knowledge we possess is worthy of the same love we offer to God.

When we think something is wonderful—whether it's a video game, a book, a friend, or a restaurant—we want to share it with others. That's what praise is like in the Bible. Hannah bragged about God's greatness: "There is no one holy like the Lord; there is no one besides you; there is no Rock like our God" (1 Samuel 2:2). David did too: "I will give thanks to you, Lord, with all my heart; I will tell of all your wonderful deeds. I will be glad and rejoice in you; I will sing the praises of your name, O Most High" (Psalm 9:1–2).

God is our good, loving, and perfect Father. We're his children, and it's good for us to brag about our heavenly Dad. We can celebrate the beauty of who God is and what he's done for us. The Father sent his Son to redeem us. If we belong to him, then our hearts naturally want to love and worship him. When we pray "hallowed be your name," we're asking him to give us joy in his goodness and to help us share his greatness with others!

THINK ABOUT IT

- What does it look like to praise God when you are by yourself?
- What does it look like to praise God when you are with others?

>>> **PRAY:** *Father, thank you for putting your holiness on display, for being a loving Father who we can trust. Help us to celebrate your glory above all else in our lives. Amen.*

What are we asking when we pray, "Your kingdom come"?

That we might see everyone have life with God under the rule of God.

MEMORY VERSE:
Again he said, "What shall we say the kingdom of God is like, or what parable shall we use to describe it? It is like a mustard seed, which is the smallest of all seeds on earth. Yet when planted, it grows and becomes the largest of all garden plants, with such big branches that the birds can perch in its shade." Mark 4:30–32

Power-up Question:
If you had to design a kingdom, what would it be like? Who and what would be there?

>>> READ MATTHEW 6:10 AND MARK 4:30-32

Rule us by your Word and Spirit in such a way that more and more we submit to you. —Heidelberg Catechism

In *Mega Man 5*, Mega Man fights through an anti-gravity facility to face up with Gravity Man. Completing the level involves playing through a fairly normal scrolling video game level, except there's one catch. For most of the level you're playing upside down. Each time you jump or climb a ladder, you're moving in the opposite direction from what you'd expect. It takes some getting used to.

When Jesus came to earth, he announced that he was building a new kingdom. But Jesus's kingdom was different from what his people expected. God's people expected the new kingdom to involve raising money, fighting large military battles, and then providing gifts for everyone in the nation. They expected the new king to live in a grand palace, wear royal robes, and be wealthy.

Jesus was not what they expected. Jesus wasn't born into riches or power. He was poor. He didn't have a grand palace. In fact, he had no place to lay his head. Jesus didn't raise money or build an army. He didn't have grandeur, wealth, or military might. His kingdom was built through quiet repentance and acts of love. Like a small seed or yeast in dough, his kingdom was so small at first that it could hardly be seen.

Like a small mustard seed grows into one of the largest garden plants, Jesus's kingdom began in humility, but it has grown to be the largest and greatest of all kingdoms (Matthew 13:31–32). Christ's kingdom began with his death for us upon the cross, but Jesus won by losing. Now people from every tribe, nation, and language find shelter with him.

So, when we pray, "Your kingdom come," we shouldn't be surprised if Christ answers in unexpected, upside-down ways. He'll rarely answer us with grand displays of power. Instead, our heavenly Father simply gives us life by his Holy Spirit so that by his grace we'll believe his holy Word and obey him more and more. When we pray, "Your kingdom come," we're praying that he would preserve his church and make it grow all over the world so that everyone will witness his kingly rule.

THINK ABOUT IT

• How have you seen God at work in unexpected, upside-down ways in your church or family?

>>> **PRAY:** *Father, bring your unexpected, upside-down kingdom in the way we live and obey you today. Amen.*

What are we asking when we pray, "Your will be done"?

That the sinfulness and brokenness of this world will be wiped away as the Spirit helps people obey God.

MEMORY VERSE:
But let justice roll on like a river, righteousness like a never-failing stream. Amos 5:24

Power-up Question:
Have you ever made a mess that you couldn't clean up?

>>> READ EZEKIEL 36:22-28 AND REVELATION 21:5

> *It is a prayer, that God may remove all the obstinacy of men, which rises in unceasing rebellion against him, and may render them gentle and submissive, that they may not wish or desire anything but what pleases him.* —John Calvin

It's so satisfying to start up a power washer and point it at a grimy patio, dirty sidewalk, or discolored fence. Line by line, you blast the filth away, making whatever you're cleaning look brand new. This work is so fulfilling that a company developed an online video game called *Power Washer Simulator*, and people can't get enough of it. Deep inside all of us, we have a desire for things to be made new. This digital cleaning adventure gives us a taste of the work we long to see God do in the real world. This is what we're asking when we pray, "Your will be done."

When our first parents rebelled against God, the whole creation fell. Sin infected all people after Adam and Eve, and it tarnished everything. Both the world and our hearts are covered with sin and brokenness we can't wash off. In our pride, we follow Adam and Eve's rebellion, thinking we know what's best instead of following God's will. Instead of trusting his plan to set things right, we try to clean ourselves. We scrub and scrub with our good works and rule-following, but we can never get the stain of sin off our hearts. Only God can heal us. Only God can repair our broken world.

How will the world be healed? By God's will. God promises that he'll make all things new. When we trust him, he replaces our hearts of stone with soft hearts of flesh (Ezekiel 36:22–28). The Spirit gives his people new desires. In Christ, we inherit a hope that God will "swallow up death" and "wipe away the tears from all faces" (Isaiah 25:8). We pray and long for the day when God's will is fulfilled in all his people. On that day, we will rejoice in the fullness of his salvation.

THINK ABOUT IT

• What do you long for God to make new?

>>> **PRAY:** *Father, thank you for your promise to make all things new. Help us to trust your will instead of our own. Amen.*

What are we asking when we pray, "Give us today our daily bread"?

That God will take care of our daily needs.

MEMORY VERSE:
"Therefore I tell you, do not worry about your life, what you will eat or drink; or about your body, what you will wear. Is not life more than food, and the body more than clothes?" Matthew 6:25

Power-up Question:
Sonic chases rings. Mario chases mushrooms. What are some of your daily needs?

>>> READ MATTHEW 6:11, 25-34

> *The more I am in a position to be tried in faith with reference to my body, my family, my service for the Lord, my business, etc., the more shall I have opportunity of seeing God's help and deliverance.*
> —George Müller

In the Sonic games, the speedy blue hedgehog must find golden rings to survive. The rings give Sonic the ability to sustain his health. But if Sonic gets hurt, he can lose all of his rings and the game. It's tempting to worry when you begin to run low on rings. But the best strategy in the game is to keep running and stay alert. The game's designers have put more rings out there with Sonic's name on them. They're just waiting to be collected.

When we pray, "Give us this day our daily bread," we're asking God to sustain us, to take care of us, and to supply our needs. Maybe you've never had to worry about whether you'll have clothes to wear, a roof over your head, or food to eat. But even if it seems like all your needs are met, this prayer reminds us that it's God who sustains us.

We depend on God's provision. The air we breathe, food we eat, and bed we sleep in are all gifts from him, so God wants us to come to him humbly and gratefully every day. He wants us to ask for what we need even if we don't feel like we're in need. He wants to remind us that every good and perfect gift comes from him, so that we don't depend on ourselves, but trust him.

Praying "Give us this day our daily bread" is a reminder that God is a loving Father who wants to care for his children. When we worry and doubt that we'll have enough, we can cast all of our anxieties on him, knowing that he cares for us (1 Peter 5:7).

THINK ABOUT IT

• When do you feel most worried? Take time to share those worries with God.

>>> PRAY: *Father, give us this day our daily bread. Help us to trust that you are our provider, that you care for us. Amen.*

What are we asking when we pray, "Forgive us our debts"?

That we receive God's forgiveness for sin and that God will enable us to forgive others.

MEMORY VERSE:

"For if you forgive other people when they sin against you, your heavenly Father will also forgive you. But if you do not forgive others their sins, your Father will not forgive your sins." Matthew 6:14–15

Power-up Question:

When you're down to your last life, how does it affect the way you play a game?

>>> READ MATTHEW 6:12 AND 18:21-35

> *You forgot I gave these also; Would you leave the best behind?*
> —*Victor Hugo*, Les Miserables

In older arcade games, it's common for players to begin with three lives—three chances to win the game. When you use up all your chances, the game is game over. Similarly, in Jewish culture, it was common to forgive another person up to three times (Job 33:29–30; Amos 1:3; 2:6). But if you sinned against a friend a fourth time, your chances for a positive relationship were slim.

In Matthew 18, Peter asks Jesus, "How many times should I forgive my brother or sister who sins against me? Up to seven times?" Jesus answers, "No, not seven, but seventy-seven times." Then Jesus shares a story about God's kingdom.

In Jesus's story, there was a man who owed millions and millions of dollars' worth of gold to a king. One day, the king came to collect what he was owed, but the man didn't have all the money. So the king ordered that the man, his wife, his children, and all he owned be sold to repay the debt. The man fell to his knees and begged, "O king, please be patient with me! I promise to pay you back every last penny." The king had compassion on the debtor and showed him mercy. Amazingly, he canceled the man's debt and set this man free.

Soon after, the same man met one of his co-workers who owed him a hundred dollars' worth of silver. The co-worker didn't have the money to pay him. Did the man show him mercy? Did he show the same compassion the king showed him? No, he spoke harshly to the man, and he put him in prison. When the king heard this, he was furious. How could this man receive so much mercy and refuse to show it to others?

Our sin leaves us with a debt to God that we cannot pay. But when Jesus died on the cross and took the punishment for our sin, he paid our debt in full. Because he has forgiven us so much, we can forgive others, too.

THINK ABOUT IT

- Do you find it challenging to forgive others? Why?
- Who might God be prompting you to forgive?

>>> PRAY: *Father, help us to forgive others as you have forgiven us in Jesus. Amen.*

What are we asking when we pray, "Lead us not into temptation but deliver us from the evil one"?

That God will keep us from sin and Satan's lies

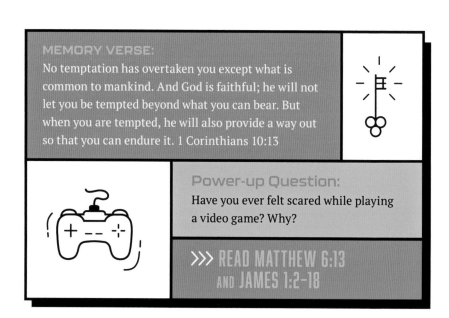

MEMORY VERSE:
No temptation has overtaken you except what is common to mankind. And God is faithful; he will not let you be tempted beyond what you can bear. But when you are tempted, he will also provide a way out so that you can endure it. 1 Corinthians 10:13

Power-up Question:
Have you ever felt scared while playing a video game? Why?

>>> READ MATTHEW 6:13 AND JAMES 1:2–18

> *And though this world with devils filled should threaten to undo us.*
> *We cannot fail for God hath willed his truth to triumph through us.*
> *—Martin Luther, "A Mighty Fortress"*

One of the coolest things about *Minecraft* is the day/night cycle. When the sun is up, you can explore, build, and farm. But when the sun goes down and the light dwindles, things can get a little scary. Zombies and skeletons hunt you, and creepers are determined to explode and destroy everything you've built. Thankfully, all you need to keep them away is a little light. Drop a torch, lantern, or campfire and the light they provide keeps the evil away. If you walk away from that warm glow, you're back in danger of being attacked. But inside the light, you are safe.

In this final part of the Lord's Prayer, Jesus reminds us of two things. First, Satan is real, and he wants to destroy us. He wants to draw us away from the light of Christ into the darkness of temptation. The devil lays traps, speaks lies, and attempts to trick us into walking away from God. Our destruction is his joy. He doesn't have to send monsters. No, his battle plan is to deceive us. He speaks doubts ("God doesn't care about you") and lies ("It's fine to give into temptation") to tempt our sinful hearts into turning away from God's Word and following after sin.

With this prayer, Jesus reminds us that God has the power to protect us and keep us safe from Satan and his schemes. The Father has given us the truth in his Word and the Holy Spirit to help us fight temptation (John 14:15–17). The truth of God's Word exposes Satan's lies, and the Spirit gives us the power to say no to temptation and sin. When we ask God to protect us from sin, he is faithful to light a torch and let us rest safe in his presence.

THINK ABOUT IT

- Are you aware when you're being tempted to sin?
- In what ways is Satan trying to trick or deceive you?

>>> PRAY: *Father, thank you for loving us and protecting us from Satan's lies. Help us to rely on the Spirit's power as we fight temptation. Amen.*

When will God's mission in the world be complete?

When Jesus returns, we will appear with him—changed into his likeness and totally free from sin.

What has Jesus prepared for his church?

Jesus prepares new bodies and a new home for his people so they live with him forever.

MEMORY VERSE:
"And if I go and prepare a place for you, I will come back and take you to be with me that you also may be where I am." John 14:3

Power-up Question:
How do you feel when you're on the verge of winning a game?

>>> READ 1 THESSALONIANS 4:13-17

There's nothing quite like the feeling you get when you complete the final level of a game. All the time, energy, and emotions (good and bad) you've invested have led to this moment. At times, you might have felt like giving up. But you kept going, knowing there was an end in sight. And now that you're done, you have a sense of accomplishment and satisfaction.

When God's mission in the world is finally complete, it will be a day of rejoicing! The Bible tells us that we will know the glorious day has arrived, because "the Lord himself will come down from heaven, with a loud command, with the voice of the archangel and with the trumpet call of God" (1 Thessalonians 4:16). Jesus will come and bring the gifts that will complete our *glorification*, the final stage of his saving work.

When Jesus returns, all believers will be resurrected (John 6:38–40). All the followers of Christ—both those who have died and those who are living—will be raised from the dead and will receive new, glorious bodies. Our new bodies will be like Jesus's body after he was raised from the dead. We will be free from sin and sickness, and our bodies will not die.

The heavens and the earth will also be changed. Jesus told his disciples that he would prepare a place for them (John 14:3). Revelation 21 explains how we will live forever in Jesus's presence. It will be our new home, and God will live with humanity again (v. 3). It will be the perfect place. God will wipe every tear from our eyes. There will be no mourning or crying or pain anymore, because the old things will have passed away (v. 4). All that was tainted by the curse of sin will be made new.

THINK ABOUT IT

• Have you ever thought about the new heavens and new earth? How do you imagine it to be?

>>> **PRAY:** *Come quickly, Lord Jesus. Amen.*

THIS IS NOT GAME OVER

All the games you play eventually come to an end. You level up your character so they're strong enough for the final boss. You find the power-up you need to make your dash to the finish. You solve the final riddle and open the last treasure chest to end your journey. All those stories come to a close, but your faith-building story will continue long after you put down this book.

You've spent weeks—perhaps even a year—laying down a beautiful foundation of Christian faith. You've pressed into big truths about God, his creation, the kingdom he's building, his law and the gospel. You've learned about Jesus's life, death, resurrection, ascension, and return. You've explored God's grace, the church, and the mission to which God has called us. But while these truths provide an essential map for the adventure of following Christ, there's still a journey ahead. We're confident that God will be faithful to complete the good work he's begun in you (Philippians 1:6). We're confident that he'll continue to strengthen your faith.

With these big truths hidden in your heart, you are free to explore God's world, dive further into his Word, and grow to know him more deeply. You can find your place in his church, and share his glory and grace with those around you. Our prayer is that over many years, you continue to level up your faith and that you'll invite others to join you along the way. Keep pressing on. Keep building until Jesus comes again!

KEVIN HIPPOLYTE serves as director of student ministry at Sojourn Church Midtown. He's also on the board at Hope Collaborative, a trauma-sensitive community development organization serving students, internationals, and neighbors. He lives with his wife, Kelly, and their son in Louisville, Kentucky.

JARED KENNEDY is an editor for The Gospel Coalition and the cofounder of Gospel-Centered Family. He is the author of *Keeping Your Children's Ministry on Mission*, *God Made Me for Worship*, and *The Beginner's Gospel Story Bible*. He and his wife, Megan, and their three girls also attend Sojourn Church Midtown.

TREY KULLMAN served for more than five years as a family pastor and is now managing editor of Gospel-Centered Family. He and his wife, Annie, and their three children also live in Louisville, Kentucky where they attend Sojourn Church J-town.

Together, the authors host Gospel-Centered Family's *Press Pause* podcast.

TRUTHFORLIFE®

THE BIBLE-TEACHING MINISTRY OF **ALISTAIR BEGG**

The mission of Truth For Life is to teach the Bible with clarity and relevance so that unbelievers will be converted, believers will be established, and local churches will be strengthened.

Daily Program

Each day, Truth For Life distributes the Bible teaching of Alistair Begg across the U.S. and in several locations outside of the U.S. through 2,000 radio outlets. To find a radio station near you, visit **truthforlife.org/stationfinder.**

Free Teaching

The daily program, and Truth For Life's entire teaching library of over 3,000 Bible-teaching messages, can be accessed for free online at **truthforlife.org** and through Truth For Life's mobile app, which can be downloaded for free from your app store.

At-Cost Resources

Books and audio studies from Alistair Begg are available for purchase at cost, with no markup. Visit **truthforlife.org/store.**

Where to Begin?

If you're new to Truth For Life and would like to know where to begin listening and learning, find starting point suggestions at **truthforlife.org/firststep.** For a full list of ways to connect with Truth For Life, visit **truthforlife.org/subscribe.**

Contact Truth For Life

P.O. Box 398000 Cleveland, Ohio 44139

phone 1 (888) 588-7884 **email** letters@truthforlife.org truthforlife.org

After learning each catechism question and answer, place a sticker where it belongs on the corresponding level map to track your progress.

LEVEL 1
GOD'S GLORY

1-1   1-2

1-3   1-4   1-5   1-6   1-7   1-8   1-9

LEVEL 2
GOD'S KINGDOM

2-1   2-2   2-3   2-4   2-5

2-6   2-7   2-8   2-9   2-10   2-11   2-12

2-13   2-14

LEVEL 3
THE GOSPEL

3-1   3-2   3-3

3-4   3-5   3-6   3-7

LEVEL 4
GOD'S GRACE

4-1

4-2   4-3   4-4   4-5   4-6   4-7   4-8

LEVEL 5
GOD'S CHURCH AND MISSION

5-1   5-2   5-3   5-4

5-5   5-6   5-7   5-8   5-9   5-10   5-11

5-12   5-13   5-14